NELSON MANDELA

Recent Titles in Greenwood Biographies

NELSON MANDELA

A Biography

Peter Limb

GREENWOOD BIOGRAPHIES

GREENWOOD PRESS
WESTPORT, CONNECTICUT • LONDON

Library of Congress Cataloging-in-Publication Data

Limb, Peter.
   Nelson Mandela : a biography / Peter Limb.
       p. cm. — (Greenwood biographies, ISSN 1540–4900)
   Includes bibliographical references and index.
   ISBN 978–0–313–34035–2 (alk. paper)
  1. Mandela, Nelson, 1918–   2. Presidents—South Africa—Biography.
  I. Title.
   DT1974.L56   2008
   968.06'5092—dc22
   [B]   2007039787

British Library Cataloguing in Publication Data is available.

Library of Congress Catalog Card Number: 2007039787
ISBN: 978–0–313–34035–2
ISSN: 1540–4900

First published in 2008

Greenwood Press, 88 Post Road West, Westport, CT 06881
An imprint of Greenwood Publishing Group, Inc.
www.greenwood.com

Printed in the United States of America

The paper used in this book complies with the
Permanent Paper Standard issued by the National
Information Standards Organization (Z39.48–1984).

10 9 8 7 6 5 4 3 2 1

For Nicole, and all those who,
like Nelson Mandela, opposed apartheid

CONTENTS

Photo essay follows page 62

SERIES FOREWORD

In response to high school and public library needs, Greenwood developed this distinguished series of full-length biographies specifically for student use. Prepared by field experts and professionals, these engaging biographies are tailored for high school students who need challenging yet accessible biographies. Ideal for secondary school assignments, the length, format, and subject areas are designed to meet educators' requirements and students' interests.

Greenwood offers an extensive selection of biographies spanning all curriculum-related subject areas including social studies, the sciences, literature and the arts, history and politics, as well as popular culture, covering public figures and famous personalities from all time periods and backgrounds, both historical and contemporary, who have made an impact on American and/or world culture. Greenwood biographies are chosen based on comprehensive feedback from librarians and educators. Consideration is given to both curriculum relevance and inherent interest. The result is an intriguing mix of the well known and the unexpected, the saints and sinners from long-ago history and contemporary pop culture. Readers will find a wide array of subject choices from fascinating crime figures like Al Capone to inspiring pioneers like Margaret Mead, from the greatest minds of our time like Stephen Hawking to the most amazing success stories of our day like J. K. Rowling.

Although the emphasis is on fact, not glorification, the books are meant to be fun to read. Each volume provides in-depth information about the subject's life from birth through childhood, the teen years, and adulthood. A thorough account relates family background and education, traces personal and professional influences, and explores struggles, accomplishments, and contributions. A timeline highlights the most significant life events against a historical perspective. Bibliographies supplement the reference value of each volume.

INTRODUCTION

Nelson Mandela is the most famous African today. His amazing roller-coaster ride to freedom after 27 years in apartheid prisons to become president of the new "rainbow nation" of South Africa is now legendary. Equally impressive is his successful reconciliation of a deadly conflict seen by many commentators as intractable.

In the period of transition from apartheid to democratic rule, and again as South Africa's first black president from 1994 to 1999, Mandela brought together bitter enemies and unified a nation. He did this by leading from example with a lack of bitterness at his own long years of imprisonment under the apartheid system, and by patiently listening to all sides of the political spectrum, a trait typical of the wise African ruler that he was.

How and why was Nelson Mandela able to carry out such major achievements? What was the secret of his "Madiba Magic"? What were his motivations? What was the impact on his personal life and his family? What is his legacy today?

To understand Mandela one needs to appreciate the rich context of his life and times. One needs to appreciate his culture, the influence of family, friends, and schools, and the power of the white settler society of South Africa and the regime of apartheid it spawned. Important too are the peoples he worked with and the movement to which he dedicated his life. To all this, insights into his character and personality, strengths and weaknesses, and the national and global forces of his time are needed finally to gain a comprehensive appraisal of his life's work.

Mandela sacrificed much to the struggle for freedom in South Africa, including his very liberty as well as his private life. The goal of African freedom always was his inspiration. His political movement, the African National Congress, was his support base and vehicle throughout his very long political career of more than 50 years. In this regard, he was the quintessential "organizational man," able to build on earlier African political structures to achieve impressive gains. He also was an innovator, an initiator of bold new directions, willing to take political risks. However, in many ways Mandela does not resemble the stereotypical political leader. Like an earlier subject of this Greenwood Biographies series, Archbishop Desmond Tutu, Mandela is a humble man of great dignity and humor, example, tolerance, and forgiveness. Both men won the Nobel Peace Prize.

Yet even more than Tutu, Mandela in his enforced prison seclusion of 27 years was *the* living legend, *the* symbol of African resistance to apartheid. For decades, people at home and abroad could neither hear his voice nor see his image; such was the power of his personality and message that the apartheid regime banned even his photograph and voice.

Mandela would be the first to agree that he and many, many other anti-apartheid leaders and supporters *combined* to remove the apartheid regime, but Mandela stood at the apex of this resistance: the general, the organizer, the African King, the "Father of the Nation" capable of realizing momentous social change. Mandela, with his tremendously physical presence, was a man of action willing to take up armed struggle in defense of the freedom and liberty of his people. Even Mandela's enemies and jailers admired his unflinching courage and dedication. He won a national and global stature equal to none in a period when political leaders have disenchanted many people.

Mandela was able to rise above the rigid constraints of the virulent racism of apartheid and the intense bitterness it engendered in many people, but he also was a product of his time and had to face apartheid's equally bitter social and economic legacy. He faced this head-on and laid down a democratic constitutional and political framework seen by many as the most progressive in the world today, and which set a new path for South Africans. Although global and national forces delayed the realization of some of his dreams, Mandela (or "Madiba" as many South Africans affectionately know him), even after his term as president, remained remarkably active in his late 80s, speaking out for human rights and for action against acute social problems.

In the pages to follow, a well-rounded, balanced view of Mandela set squarely in his time and place is presented. Woven into the biographical narrative are cultural, social, political, and personal forces to let the reader see Mandela in his full complexity, even majesty, and also to share his hopes, his victories and defeats, his despair, and his joy, through his own words and deeds and those of his closest companions and compatriots. Nelson Mandela is quite simply one of the greatest leaders, and personalities, in world history.

TIMELINE OF EVENTS IN THE LIFE OF NELSON MANDELA

July 18, 1918	Birth of Nelson Mandela in Mvezo, the Transkei, South Africa
1920	Family moves to Qunu village
1926	Starts elementary school; given the name "Nelson" by teacher
1927	Death of father; Mandela moves to royal court of Thembu Chief Jongintaba Dalindyebo at Mqhekez-weni
1934	Initiation
1935	Starts secondary education at Clarkebury school
1937	Higher schooling at Healdtown prep school
1939	Studies at University College of Fort Hare
November 1940	Is forced to leave Fort Hare after student protests
April 1941	Leaves for Johannesburg to avoid arranged marriage
1941	Works in Johannesburg; lives in Alexandra; meets Walter Sisulu
1942	Makes contact with the African National Congress (ANC)
December 1942	Receives Bachelor of Arts degree from Fort Hare
1943	Begins legal studies; joins Alexandra bus boycott
1944	Marries Evelyn Mase
April 1944	Congress Youth League is formed; Mandela is a founder
August 1946	African mine workers' strike

1947	Elected to Transvaal ANC executive committee
1948	National Party government elected and starts to implement apartheid
1949	ANC adopts Program of Action
1950	Joins ANC National Executive
1951	Elected Youth League president
1952	Defiance Campaign; Mandela arrested, then banned; becomes president of Transvaal ANC, deputy president of ANC; qualifies as attorney
1953	Opposes Sophiatown forced removals; opens legal practice
1955	Congress of the People adopts the Freedom Charter
December 5, 1956	Charged with treason
January 1957	Evelyn and Mandela separate
June 14, 1958	Marries Nomzamo Winifred Madikizela
March 21, 1960	Sharpeville Massacre of 69 Africans by police
April 8, 1960	ANC and Pan Africanist Congress (PAC) banned
March 29, 1961	Mandela and others accused of treason acquitted
May 1961	Organizes "stay-at-home" protests
December 16, 1961	Launches sabotage campaign
January–July 1962	Travels widely in Africa and to England to gain support
August 5, 1962	Arrested inside South Africa
November 1962	Sentenced to three years prison
1963–1964	Rivonia Trial
April 20, 1964	Delivers famous speech from the dock
June 12, 1964	Sentenced to life imprisonment; sent to Robben Island
1969	Winnie Mandela held in prison for 491 days
1976	Refuses conditional release
June 16, 1976	Student protests in Soweto; countrywide revolt develops
May 17, 1977	Winnie Mandela banished to rural town of Brandfort
March 31, 1982	Transferred to Pollsmoor Prison
August 20, 1983	United Democratic Front (UDF) formed

January 1984	Refuses conditional release, and daughter Zindzi reads his defiant response at rally; allowed first contact visit with Winnie
1985	State of emergency; initiates secret talks with government
May 1986	Meets Commonwealth Eminent Persons' Group
October 2, 1986	U.S. Congress passes Comprehensive Anti-Apartheid Act
1987–1988	Meetings with government representatives
December 9, 1988	Transferred to Victor Verster Prison
August 14, 1989	F. W. de Klerk succeeds P. W. Botha as state president
February 2, 1990	F. W. de Klerk lifts ban on ANC
February 11, 1990	Released from prison after 27 years
March 2, 1990	Reappointed ANC deputy president
March 1990	Visits Zambia and Sweden to meet ANC's exiled leadership
May–August 1990	ANC–government talks lead to suspension of armed struggle and release of some political prisoners
June 1990	Tours Europe, North America, and Africa
July 5, 1991	Elected ANC president
December 1991	Congress for a Democratic South Africa (CODESA) opens
April 1992	Separation from Winnie
May 1992	ANC withdraws from CODESA after "third force" violence
September 1992	Negotiations resume with government
April 1993	South African Communist Party (SACP) leader Chris Hani assassinated; Mandela calls for calm
December 10, 1993	Receives, with F.W. de Klerk, the Nobel Peace Prize
April 26–28, 1994	ANC wins decisive 62.6 percent victory at first democratic elections
May 10, 1994	Mandela inaugurated as South Africa's first black president
December 1994	Autobiography, *Long Walk to Freedom*, launched
December 1995	Truth and Reconciliation Commission appointed
1996	New constitution adopted

March 1996	Divorces Winnie
July 18, 1998	Marries Graça Machel
June 2, 1999	ANC wins second term; steps down as president
December 1999	Diplomatic role facilitating peace talks in Burundi
January 2005	Announces death of son Makgatho, from AIDS
2006	After voicing criticisms of government, retires from public life
July 18, 2007	Aged 89, announces formation of the Elders group

Chapter 1

FAMILY AND CHILDHOOD

Nelson Mandela's childhood and family background helped shape his personality and the views that would be so evident in his later life. Mandela's own memories and feelings about his childhood, as related in his autobiography, show how influential—at one level—were these years.

Mandela's birthplace was the small South African rural village of Mvezo in the district of Qunu. Although the house in which he was born no longer exists, this beautiful village still exists today, not very far from the town of Umtata (Mthatha) in the region known as the Transkei (literally, across the Kei River). The Mandela homestead overlooked the Mbashe (Bashee) River.

At first glance, this landscape seems so tranquil: gurgling unpolluted rivers run through rolling hills inhabited by livestock tended by boy-shepherds. This is the heartland of the Thembu people, an important section of the Xhosa nation. Here Rolihlahla Madiba Dalibhunga Mandela, later known the world over as Nelson Mandela, was born on July 18, 1918.

In these pastoral surroundings, Mandela learned from his family and clan about his people's culture and traditions. Later, he would attend English-language, European-style schools, but as a child, he fully imbibed Xhosa culture, its language, initiation customs, and ideas of leadership and humanness or *ubuntu* (a feeling of fellowship and compassion in African society). His given name, Rolihlahla, translates literally as "one who pulls branches from a tree," or simply "troublemaker." His clan name Madiba ("reconciler") would remain a "praise name" and term of affection used by friends and compatriots in years to come.[1]

Many African cultures feature extended family structures, with sons and daughters of uncles and aunts considered as brothers and sisters, not cousins. Mandela's extended family was no exception. His sister Mabel Notancu Ntimakhwe, when interviewed in the 1980s and 1990s, recalled Rolihlahla as a serious young boy even then, with "leadership qualities," and whom people recognized as bright. Another, younger, sister, Leabie, remembers that at the time his sisters called him "Buti."[2]

Another important feature of Xhosa society was respect for the elders. Such features of African culture, involving a commitment to wider social well-being and deference to established leadership, would be recurring themes in Mandela's adult life, not least because of his own social status as an integral member of the Xhosa royalty.[3]

Mandela's father, Gadla Henry Mphakanyiswa (1880–1927) was chief councilor to the paramount chief (or king) of the Thembu people. Xhosa nobility have three "Houses," a Great House from which rulers are traced, the Right Hand House, and a minor or Left Hand House. Mandela was born into the Right Hand House and in this regard was very much part of the Xhosa royal family, although his descent-line was not that of the ruler. Moreover, he was only the youngest of four sons. However Gadla, as chief advisor to the king, played an important part in decisions, notably in a royal succession dispute in 1924 that was to have an important bearing on Nelson Mandela's life. Gadla was headman of Mvezo village, in which capacity he chaired community meetings and local ceremonies. He also served in the Bhunga, a purely advisory council overseen by the white government. Given this social prominence, Rolihlahla's father was a custodian of Thembu and Xhosa history, and he imparted to his son many stirring narratives of African history. Rolihlahla also inherited his father's tall and proud bearing.

Mandela's mother, Nonqaphi Nosekeni Fanny, was the third of his father's four wives. Xhosa men would take more than one wife in accordance with their prosperity, also indicated by the number of cattle they owned, cattle being the most important form of wealth, used for bride wealth, or dowry payment, upon marriage. Nosekeni had an important formative influence on her son. Mandela later recalled that his mother was his "first real friend."[4] She related to him Xhosa moral tales and legends and, after becoming a Christian and taking the name "Fanny," she duly ensured that the Methodist (Wesleyan) Church baptized her son.

Mandela had three sisters, Baliwe, Notancu (Mabel), and Makhutswana. His father also had three sons and six daughters by other wives. As a boy, Mandela delighted in playing with them traditional games and sports, such as stick-fighting, riding animals, and making toys. The stick-fighting game of boys encouraged a sense of honor or magnanimity in victory without dishonoring an opponent, a principle that would guide Mandela in later life: "I learned that to humiliate another person is to make him suffer an unnecessarily cruel fate. Even as a boy, I defeated my opponents without dishonoring them."[5]

However, these bucolic surroundings of the Transkei where Mandela grew up disguised deeper troubles about which he would soon learn: land dispossession, colonization, and racism. By the time he was born, Africans no longer owned most of the land, which white settlers now controlled. African women largely worked the land, with their men forced into long and dangerous shifts of migrant labor on the distant gold mines of Johannesburg to be able to pay taxes to the white government. In his early years, rural life effectively quarantined Mandela from these harsh influences. Instead, he was able to learn the customs and traditions of Xhosa society. Moreover, his social status as a member of the royal line meant that he was destined for an education and not the working-class life of a miner. Nevertheless, a sudden decline of his father's material interests and the warning of elders about the lessons of South African history signaled to Mandela that his life was not likely to be easy.

African peoples had inhabited South Africa for many centuries before Dutch settlement at the Cape of Good Hope in the mid-seventeenth century. African nations included the Xhosa, Zulu, Tswana and Sotho, who spoke related languages and were largely agricultural-pastoral peoples with developed trade networks and complex cultures, as well as the more pastoral or foraging Khoikhoi and San ("Bushmen") peoples. The Dutch soon introduced slaves from Southeast Africa and Southeast Asia and, over the next century-and-a-half, steadily conquered African lands. The process of dispossession accelerated after the British took control of the Cape Colony during the Napoleonic Wars. As European armies and settlers pushed east, it was primarily the Xhosa people, with their relatively developed social and military systems, that stood in their way. The Xhosa would face more than one hundred years of warfare in a desperate attempt to hold their lands. But by the time of Mandela's father, this protracted war was lost. Gadla's own position as headman was now dependent on the whim of British officials. Still, the Xhosa lands of the Eastern Cape had by then become the center of an African revival coupled with early African nationalism as the indigenous people abandoned methods of direct resistance for mission Christianity, education, and new forms of political organization.

The long period of African resistance to European conquest and colonization influenced Mandela's father and other Xhosa elders from whom the young Nelson would learn this history. In 1920, when Mandela was only two years of age, came a bolt of lightning; the government deposed his father as headman for alleged insubordination over the small matter of a local dispute among villagers about a stray ox. His father saw the dispute as essentially one in his own domain, of traditional, chiefly, jurisprudence. As a matter of principle, he refused to acknowledge white power in this sphere. In this regard, Gadla was following precedent: the Thembu Paramount Chief, Dalindyebo (1865–1923), had long intervened in local resource conflicts to challenge white authority. In Mandela's own words, his father was "asserting his traditional prerogative as a chief" and displaying "a proud rebelliousness, a stubborn sense of injustice"—which Mandela believes he inherited.[6]

As a result, the Mandela family lost most of its land and cattle and had to move to a larger village, Qunu, for the support of kin. Gadla's act of brave, if futile resistance was all the more remarkable given the complex recent history of the Thembu people who, as historic rivals of the central Xhosa kingdom, had been successively weakened in the nineteenth century by British "divide and rule" strategy that exploited divisions among Xhosa-speaking peoples. As a result, the Thembu had sought some kind of accommodation with both Xhosa neighbors and British invaders and they were perhaps unique among African nations in the region for retention of a good deal of their lands.

It is important to understand the centrality of the land question in South African history and how it thus impacted Mandela's life. Shared land ownership had been the basis of precolonial African society. Many years later, in 1964, Nelson Mandela would state, "The structure and organization of the original African societies of this country . . . have had a great influence on my political concepts. . . . The land, which was the primary resource in those days, belonged to the tribe as a whole. Private property did not exist." By the time of Mandela's father, there was evidence of the growth of class stratification, with chiefs holding more land and cattle than commoners, but the principle of sharing remained widespread.[7]

Gadla's action reflected rising African frustration at a time of acute political, social, economic, and environmental crises in the Transkei. In the Act of Union of 1910, when the modern nation of South Africa emerged out of the unification of four colonies, Britain ceded political power only to whites, with most blacks denied the vote. The new white government embarked on an extensive range of laws that greatly intensified racial discrimination and segregation. In particular, the Natives' Land Act of 1913 prevented blacks, who comprised more than 80 percent of the population, from freely buying land and progressively restricted them to live in the least fertile 13 percent of the country. By World War I, many Thembu enlisted in the British Empire armed forces in the hope of achieving greater equality at home and abroad, but they were sorely disappointed when denied even the right to carry arms. After the war, discrimination, far from lessening, increased.

Having lost much of their land and all their political power, Africans now lost control over their very livelihoods, with most of the men from Mandela's village forced into migrant labor hundreds of miles away on the gold mines. At the same time, African access to land and forests was increasingly restricted,[8] while prices rose sharply after the war with no commensurate increase in black wages. To add to their woes, an influenza epidemic decimated the population. Culturally, the government denied Africans the right to practice many of their traditional customs. All these factors help explain the action of Mandela's father in challenging white authority and set the stage for the development of Mandela's own ideas.

Despite his father's loss of income and land, Rolihlahla recalls his time in Qunu as the "happiest years of my boyhood." He played with other children, herded cattle, became adept at stick fighting, and enjoyed sliding down huge, smooth rocks with other boys. Yet great changes in his life were afoot. It was in Qunu at the age of seven that Mandela, prompted by his Christian mother and family friend George Mbekela, first went to school—the first member of his family to do so. He was enrolled in a single-room mission school where his elementary school teacher, Ms. Mdingane, gave him a British name, Nelson, that stuck. He had to wear his father's clothes, cut down to size, and his sister Mabel remembers that whereas other children laughed at his scarecrow appearance, Mandela "was determined to get an education." His education, he later recalled, was one "in which British ideas, British institutions, were automatically assumed to be superior. There was no such thing [to the authorities] as African culture." Even at this early age, recollects Mabel, Mandela was quick to come to the aid of other people. Once he helped fix the motorbike of a young white man, who paid him for the favor. She remembers too that the girls with whom he sometimes played were older sisters from the senior house.[9]

Not long afterwards, in 1927 at the age of nine, Mandela experienced another sharp change in his life as he saw his father die of lung disease. He left his mother and moved to the "Great Place" of Mqhekezweni, home of the Paramount Chief of Thembuland. A few years earlier in a succession dispute and with the then Paramount Chief Sabata too young to rule, Mandela's father in his role as royal councilor had ruled in favor of Jongintaba (David Dalindyebo) to serve as regent. Jongintaba, also a member of the Madiba clan, now returned the favor, agreeing to become guardian of Gadla's son.

Jongintaba groomed Mandela as a future royal councilor. The chief's wife No-England adopted him as virtually her own son. Mandela grew up with the regent's son, Justice, four years his senior and already active in sports, acting as a close and loving brother and mentor. At the Great Place, Mandela enjoyed the company of his new brother. He also played with Noma, Jongintaba's daughter, and Ntombizodwa, the daughter of a cousin of Jongintaba, who in the 1980s recollected Nelson as "very well behaved and respectful of all the elders," as well as "diligent and hardworking both with his studies and with the chores that were assigned to him at the Great Place." Life was not always easy in rural Mqhekezweni; for instance, it lacked electricity. Nevertheless, many years later Mandela still treasured how Jongintaba had raised him as his own son.[10]

Mandela's years at the Great Place impressed upon him the African tradition of leadership and conflict resolution through consensus—"democracy in its purest form" as he later characterized it. At village meetings, every (male) person was entitled to speak, with the chief not above criticism and ruling only after patiently hearing all views. Mandela learned the techniques of how to become a leader from Jongintaba and elders at the royal court. The aged Chief Zwelibhangile Joyi taught him about African history and dispossession of the Thembu at the hands of the *abelungu* (whites). Mandela recalled, "As a leader, I have always followed the principles I first saw demonstrated by the regent at the Great Place." He continued to attend a Methodist mission elementary school, studying English, Xhosa, history, and geography, and now regularly attended church with the regent, who later enrolled him in another, higher school at Qokolweni, personally driving him there in his much-prized Ford V8 automobile.[11]

In 1934, at the age of 16, Mandela underwent Thembu initiation rituals to prove his courage so he could make the transition to manhood. The circumcision ceremony, still practiced although in different forms today, occurred at the sacred Thembu royal initiation place of Tyhalarha on the banks of the Mbashe River, secluded from women. The ritual included daubing of the body with white clay and the wearing of special clothing made from natural fibers, and the removal of the foreskin was performed with an *assegai* (spear) with no anesthetic: Mandela still remembers the pain that caused him to delay calling out *Ndiyindoda* ("I am a man") to affirm his manhood after the ceremony.

The new name given to Mandela after the ritual was "Dalibhunga" or "founder of the Bhunga," which given his later political leadership, would prove prophetic. Although not yet a "political animal," his interest in such matters awakened when, during the ritual, Chief Meligqili addressed the initiates, or *abakhwetha*. Despite the promise of manhood in the ceremony, the chief warned the initiates that this was in reality an illusion:

> For we Xhosas, and all Black South Africans, are a conquered people. We are slaves in our own country. We are tenants on our own soil. We have no strength, no power, no control over our own destiny in the land of our birth. They [the initiates] will go to cities where they will live in shacks . . . and cough their lungs out in the bowels of the white man's mines, destroying their health, never seeing the sun, so that the white man can live a life of unequaled prosperity."[12]

Mandela later wrote that whereas he, unlike most of the other initiates, was not destined to work in the mines, he never forgot these words so well grounded in the recent history of Africans all around the country.

After the ceremony, Mandela arranged a welcome party for his close family to mark the completion of his elementary education. He had kept in touch with his family at Qunu. Younger relative Arthur Mandela recalled in 1988 that Nelson used to visit his mother and siblings. Arthur's memories of his older relative, and how other people in the village regarded him, if perhaps a little romanticized by time, revolved around Nelson's attitudes. "It was clear that he was a leader because he had great respect for a decent education. . . . He never had any ill feeling about anyone. He was never involved in any dispute or quarrel. He was never sickly." Mandela, he noted, had a reputation for intervening in fights of others to try to resolve them amicably.[13]

Soon afterwards, Mandela left the Great Place to begin his secondary education. Many years later, when a prisoner of apartheid on the barren and isolated Robben Island, Mandela wrote nostalgically to his sister of how much he missed her and his family and the places where he was raised: "I miss Mvezo where I was born and Qunu where I spent the first ten years of my childhood. I long to see Tyalara where . . . I underwent the traditional rights of manhood. I would love to bathe once more in the water of Umbashe, as I did at the beginning of 1935." He also mentioned to his sister how Chief Jongintaba had inspired him to set goals in life.[14]

Mandela's childhood and early youth offers important insights into his later ideas and leadership style. The African traditions that Mandela learnt at Mvezo, Qunu, and Mqhekezweni emphasized kinship, hospitality, *ubuntu*, collective decision-making, reconciliation, and honor.[15] His father's resistance to white domination and the tales of black opposition to white invasion handed down by his mother and by elders inspired the young Mandela to stand up for his rights and those of his people. These feelings were strengthened as he began to witness and experience the arrogance and racism of school and government authorities. The strong collective bonds and feelings of mutual support felt among Africans across families and clans, as seen in Mandela's adoption by the Paramount Chief, would become a hallmark of Mandela's politics.[16]

Already, personality features were becoming apparent that would in years to come feature in Mandela's poise, measured speech, and common touch. Yet despite Mandela's royal upbringing and the undoubted significance of his early years, his later rise to lead the country was not predestined; indeed, over the years, the state would co-opt many African chiefs and headmen into the apartheid system. The reasons why Mandela's path would be different lie in events over the next two decades that were to catapult him into national prominence, but an inkling of the future political potency of Nelson Rolihlahla Mandela, the "troublemaker," would become apparent in his secondary and tertiary education years.

NOTES

1. Luli Callinicos, *The World That Made Mandela: A Heritage Trial* (Johannesburg: STE, 2000), p. 19.

2. Interviewed in the films *Remember Mandela!* (Vancouver: Villon Films, 1988) and *Mandela: Son of Africa, Father of a Nation* (Johannesburg: Island Pictures, 1995); Fatima Meer, *Higher than Hope: The Authorized Biography of Nelson Mandela* (New York: Harper, 1990), p. 4. Mandela has two full sisters, Mabel and Constance; Leabie was the daughter of his father's other wife.

3. Nelson Mandela, *Long Walk to Freedom: The Autobiography of Nelson Mandela* (Boston: Little, Brown, 1994), p. 8. The recent cartoon series "The Madiba Legacy Series" (Johannesburg: Nelson Mandela Foundation, 2005–2006) graphically captures Mandela's life, with the first issue, "A Son of the Eastern Cape," treating his childhood.

4. Nelson Mandela interviewed in the documentary film *Madiba: The Life and Times of Nelson Mandela* (Canada: CBC, 2004).

5. Jean Guiloineau, *The Early Life of Rolihlahla Madiba Nelson Mandela* (Berkeley, CA: North Atlantic Books, 1998), pp. 43–52; Callinicos, *The World That Made Mandela*, p. 23.

6. Mandela, *Long Walk to Freedom*, p. 6. His father was not always hostile to authority: when subheadman in 1908 he was rewarded for assisting a prosecution over use of forest products on Paramount Chief Dalindyebo's farm: Cape Archives Repository (CAR) file T 1125/3078. According to a younger relative, at the time there may also have been a dispute between Gadla and Chief Sampu: Transcript of an interview with Arthur Mandela, 1985, Qunu, Peter Davis Collection, Black Film Center, Indiana University.

7. J. B. Peires, *The House of Phalo: A History of the Xhosa People in the Days of Their Independence* (Berkeley: University of California Press, 1982), p. 87; Mandela's speech to the 1964 Rivonia Trial, cited in Guiloineau, *Early Life of Mandela*, p. 70.

8. See Jacob A. Tropp, *Natures of Colonial Change: Environmental Relations in the Making of the Transkei* (Athens: Ohio University Press, 2006), pp. 35–37.

9. Mandela, *Long Walk to Freedom*, p. 12.

10. Meer, *Higher than Hope*, p. 7; transcript of an interview with Mabel Notancu, Qunu, 1985, Peter Davis Collection, Black Film Center, Indiana University.

11. Mandela, *Long Walk to Freedom*, pp. 18–20; Meer, *Higher than Hope*, p. 8. Mandela's signed church membership cards of 1929 and 1931 are reproduced in: Nelson Mandela Foundation, *A Prisoner in the Garden* (New York: Viking Studio, 2006), p. 44.

12. Callinicos, *The World That Made Mandela*, pp. 37–39; Mandela, *Long Walk to Freedom*, p. 26. In later life, one of the few people allowed to call Mandela by his circumcision name was his Robben Island comrade Eddie Daniel: interview with E. Daniel, East Lansing, MI, September 2006, and E. Daniels, *There and Back: Robben Island 1964–1979* (Bellville: Mayibuye, 1998), p. 213.

13. Transcript of interview with Arthur Mandela, 1985, Qunu, Peter Davis Collection.

14. Handwritten letter of Mandela to his sister, reproduced in Mac Maharaj and Ahmed Kathrada, *Mandela: The Authorized Portrait* (Kansas City, MO: Andrews McMeel, 2006), p. 19.

15. Interview with Chiefs Mtirara and Joyi by John Carlin, 1999, in *The Long Walk of Nelson Mandela*: http://www.pbs.org/wgbh/pages/frontline/shows/mandela/interviews/chiefs.html.

16. Tom Lodge, *Mandela: A Critical Life* (New York: Oxford University Press, 2006). Lodge suggests Mandela may have purposively cultivated the myth of an ordained, aristocratic, leadership role. This must remain speculative, awaiting further research, but several questions, such as why the youngest son was groomed as a councilor, remain unanswered.

Chapter 2

EDUCATION AND YOUTH

Shortly after his initiation at the age of 16, Nelson Mandela left the Great Place to begin his secondary education, a phase of his life that was to open new vistas. His schooling would have a major impact on his ideas in later life.

Mandela's first secondary school was the somewhat elite and prestigious Clarkebury Boarding Institute, situated in the nearby district of Engcobo. It was "elite" in the sense of catering for the educated black stratum, but the term "elite" in colonized South Africa could be rather misleading, for this tiny African group lacked both political power and democratic rights and increasingly was denied opportunities to accumulate wealth or land. Moreover, black educational facilities, even for the elite, were inferior to that of whites.

Mandela enrolled at Clarkebury in January 1935, once more driven there personally by the regent in his Ford V8, a symbol of enormous status among blacks at the time. By this time, things were getting steadily harder for Africans. The whites-only government was embarking on a further set of discriminatory laws that would strip Africans of their few remaining electoral rights. Two decades of harsh segregation and discriminatory laws such as the Native Urban Areas Act of 1923 and the Native Administration Act of 1927 had followed the Act of Union in 1910.

Since the mid-nineteenth century, African education had been dominated by Christian missions; there was in fact very little government involvement in or support for black education. Clarkebury was a Methodist Wesleyan mission school. School principal Reverend Cecil C. Harris was strict and aloof from the students. Yet, when Mandela happened to work in

Harris's garden he discovered—as he often was to find in his relationships across racial lines—a more human side to this, the first white man with whom he came into close contact. The experience also nurtured Mandela's love of gardening, a pastime later to be of some significance in his life.

Clarkebury mission station had been founded by Wesleyan missionaries in 1830 with a land grant from the Thembu King Ngubencuka. The mission station's educational institute, established in 1875, had developed a high reputation among Thembu people; its motto of "Lift as You Rise" was somewhat akin to those of African American colleges of the day. Three decades before Mandela attended, another Thembu youth, who like Mandela also was destined to lead the African National Congress (ANC), Alfred Bitini Xuma, had studied there.

Despite its popularity and proximity to Thembu people, the school was very much in the style of a British Empire school. English was the only language of instruction, and the curriculum was British and Christian, with no room in textbooks or lessons for African culture or African history that white society disparaged. Mandela readily admits that his education was in the British mold that groomed the black elite to be "Black Englishmen." For example, he and other pupils read and admired Shakespeare. Nevertheless, he imbibed the best of these British ideas, notably a belief in liberal democracy, justice, and chivalry, which often had echoes in African culture. As with many of his generation, Mandela typified an ambiguity toward the British Empire. Later in life, his admiration of "British" justice and democracy would become well known even if the harsh facts of colonial conquest had, as noted in the previous chapter, already been handed down to him by his elders. In a 1996 speech to the British Houses of Parliament he "gently but firmly reminded Britons . . . that it was their colonization . . . that sowed the seeds of white supremacy in South Africa."[1]

Mandela the pupil still identified very much as Thembu. In spite of meeting at the school Africans from different cultures than his own, he later confessed that then "my horizons did not extend beyond Thembuland and I believed that to be a Thembu was the most enviable thing in the world." Yet Clarkebury, like other white-run schools in South Africa, tended to looked down upon African culture, instead promoting European "civilization." Hence, the school largely ignored Mandela's ties with the Thembu royalty. As a result, he gradually began to shed some of his rural and provincial habits as his homesickness gradually gave way to a growing familiarity with urban lifestyles. At Clarkebury, now aged 17, he also made his "first true female friend," a fellow student named Mathona, although little came of the casual relationship.[2]

Mandela studied assiduously for two years at Clarkebury. He successfully completed—in two years instead of the mandated three years—what was then known as the Junior Certificate or Standard Six, Forms 1–3 (roughly middle school, or lower high school). In January 1937, in his nineteenth year, he graduated to the even more prestigious Healdtown Wesleyan College, a prep school, to study for the university-entrance examination known as matriculation.

Healdtown at the time was one of the largest African schools on the continent with some one thousand students. It is located on a high plateau in rugged but beautiful terrain of the Ciskei, six miles from the old colonial town of Fort Beaufort several hours travel to the west of Clarkebury. Cape Governor Sir George Grey had founded Healdtown in 1853, and its second principal had been the father of Olive Schreiner, famous South African novelist. Already by the turn of the century, the school was attracting African boys and girls from around the country, had prominent sporting and debating clubs, and included among its graduates some of the most prominent African leaders of the day, including John Tengu Jabavu and Silas T. Molema. In the decade before Mandela arrived, school authorities had expanded, refurbished, and modernized the buildings of burnt brick, adding new classrooms, a science block, a 600-person dining hall, double-storey dormitories, water pump, and electricity, such that Healdtown was described by an African contemporary of Mandela as "a neat self-contained township." By 1930, the institution boasted 800 students, 464 of them boarders, with 32 teachers.[3]

By 1937, when Mandela arrived, the Principal of Healdtown was the Reverend A. Arthur Wellington, who that year also served as president of the Methodist Conference of South Africa. Even more than Reverend Harris, he was a stern disciplinarian. The school operated on rigid lines, perhaps contributing to Mandela's later great self-discipline.[4]

By his own confession, Mandela had been a solid rather than brilliant student up until then, but his undoubted brightness emerged when he won a Healdtown prize in 1938 for the best Xhosa essay. He also took readily to school sports, especially boxing and long-distance running.

However, what really stuck in Mandela's memory was the visit to the college of the celebrated Xhosa bard, or *imbongi* (praise-singer), S.E.K. (Krune) Mqhayi. At the performance, the praise-singer sensationally emerged from behind a door that the African students had always presumed was reserved for whites. He then characteristically began to recite—in ways analogous to modern rap singers—his majestic poetry in the voluble oral tradition typical of many rural African societies. Mqhayi then startled Mandela by having the audacity to predict a future victory of Africans over white colonialists. Subsequently, the praise-singer symbolically called on all the nations of the world to come forth so that he could "divide the stars" among them. To the Europeans he gave the largest group of stars, the Constellation, as he said they were greedy nations, causing wars and suffering. To the House of Xhosa he gave the "the most important," the Morning Star, "the star for counting the years—the years of manhood." Mandela was greatly impressed—Mqhayi's performance was "like a comet streaking across the night sky." Mandela's Xhosa identity was reinforced; his narrow Thembu parochialism was giving way to a wider Xhosa iden-tification. However this "Xhosaness" now mixed with a growing sense of having a wider African identity—a feeling enhanced by mixing with stu-dents and teachers from a broad range of ethnic backgrounds—and, more disturbingly, with the uncertainty of being forced to live in a subservient position vis-à-vis whites.[5]

An element of segregation between white and black teachers was evi-dent at Healdtown and, as at Clarkebury, the curriculum was heavily British-oriented. Mandela still recalls how the principal boasted that he was a descendant of the famous Duke of Wellington who had saved civili-zation for Europe—and for "the natives." The persistence of "Britishness" in Mandela's Transkeian homeland—part of an otherwise independent Dominion of the British Empire—was illustrated by the 1936 visit to the region of the Governor General and extensive festivities in honor of the coronation of King George VI the following year. Yet at Healdtown, Man-dela also snatched glimpses of a rising African determination to achieve greater dignity and rights when he witnessed his chaplain and housemas-ter, the Reverend Seth Mokitimi, stand up successfully to the principal's arrogant high-handedness. Mandela would not have known it at the time, but such stirrings of African dignity would become apparent eight years later when one of his Healdtown teachers, Victor Mbobo, joined Mandela in forming the ANC Youth League.[6]

Having completed his secondary education and matriculated a year ahead of schedule, in February 1939 Mandela joined a very select group of African students who had qualified to study at the South African Native College (known later as the University College of Fort Hare, and today as the University of Fort Hare). Built around the crumbling remains of a British colonial fort of the nineteenth century and some 20 miles from Healdtown in one direction, and the picturesque Amatola Mountains in the other, the college lies near the sleepy rural town of Alice. Only a mile apart, the renowned Lovedale secondary institution, Fort Hare, and Alice comprised a convenient triangle that enabled Mandela and other students to visit the town.

Founded in 1915 after concerted fund-raising and lobbying by Africans, Fort Hare was a missionary institution run by white administrators but was interdenominational and employed some black faculty. Effectively it was the only "black" college in South Africa and therefore had great prestige and affection among Africans right across the subcontinent of Southern Africa—to Mandela, Fort Hare "was Oxford and Cambridge, Harvard and Yale, all rolled into one."[7] In the years in and around when Mandela attended, many future leaders of neighboring countries studied there.

Fort Hare was a small college of only some 150 to 200 students and "Madiba" made many new acquaintances, some of whom would become close lifetime friends. Oliver Tambo, later to be Mandela's partner in the first successful African legal firm and to lead the ANC in exile, was a year older. He came from a humble peasant background in Pondoland but had been educated in urban Johannesburg. At Fort Hare, the two students were not yet close, but they did work together out of school hours in the Student Christian Association, teaching local villagers to read.[8]

Years later, Tambo remembered Mandela as a popular, highly respected, and good-natured college student with a wide range of friends, already "famous as an athlete, and one of the foremost runners at Fort Hare." In debate, Mandela was "always cautious and calculating," and he was very sensitive to insults or racism. A somewhat closer friend at this time was a fellow Xhosa royal, Kaiser Matanzima, a nephew or distant cousin (but "brother" according to African custom), who mentored Mandela and encouraged him to stand up for his rights as an African. In later years Matanzima, as leader of the Transkei Bantustan, would become a political puppet of the apartheid regime, yet even though Mandela would strongly disapprove of such politics he nevertheless always regarded Matanzima as a family friend, indicating his own conciliatory nature and emphasis on African unity. Matanzima introduced Mandela to the sport of soccer— Mandela distinctly recalls first meeting Oliver Tambo on the soccer field at Fort Hare—but his continued preference for boxing and long-distance running over team sports hints at a strong individualism.[9]

As Mandela's social horizons widened, along with many classmates, he took up new pastimes. He practiced ballroom dancing (styling himself on the famous English dancer Victor Sylvester) and joined the Fort Hare Dramatic Society, costarring (as John Wilkes Booth) in a play about Abraham Lincoln. Mandela was, as he described himself to the writer Nadine Gordimer in 1960, a "lively minded all-rounder who threw himself into a wide variety of activities outside the lecture rooms."[10]

Fort Hare was in some ways unlike an American college. British missionaries administered it, the faculty was comprised largely of white academics, and the low fees instituted to make enrollments more accessible to the generally under-resourced black community meant that dormitory life was Spartan; the food in particular was notoriously monotonous and meager in quality. Nevertheless, by the time Mandela arrived the college had already built an impressive array of stone buildings, including Stewart Hall, a tuition block, a large dining and assembly hall, and several student hostels. Attached to the college was an agricultural experiment farm of 1,600 acres. Many of the teachers, as well as the Scottish-born principal, Alexander Kerr, had views far removed from the racist stereotypes of Africans then prevalent in white South African society.

At Fort Hare, Mandela enrolled in a Bachelor of Arts program. He studied social anthropology/African government and law (then called "Native Administration"), politics, English, and Roman Dutch law. In his second year at college, he expressed interest in becoming an interpreter in the civil service and studied this subject. Interpreting was a career at the time highly prized among Africans for its relatively good salary and status,[11] although Mandela probably also saw opportunities here for assisting his clan and fellow rural Africans—many of whom could not easily follow the legal proceedings of the day, which were conducted largely in English or Afrikaans languages.

Mandela's university teachers included the leading South African black intellectuals of the day. Professor Z. K. Matthews (1901–1968) had graduated from Fort Hare in 1924 and studied at Yale and London Universities. He returned in 1936 to lecture in anthropology. Matthews, who became a leading figure of the ANC in the 1950s, taught Mandela Native Administration and social anthropology. Mandela recalls that in lectures Matthews openly criticized the segregationist government. Another of Mandela's teachers was the equally distinguished, if more politically cautious, Davidson D. T. Jabavu (1885–1959). African students held both men in very high esteem. Both also were active in wider public work, Matthews serving as adviser to the British government over the establishment of Makerere College in Uganda and as an elected member of the Natives' Representative Council, which if a purely tokenistic advisory "toy telephone" of the government nevertheless to some extent broadly represented black opinion. Both professors were of moderate politics, emphasizing the need for gradual, peaceful constitutional change to extend full democratic rights to Africans. However, government increasingly viewed even such moderate views as a potential danger to white supremacy.[12]

The ramming through Parliament in 1935 of the discriminatory Hertzog Acts, which excluded Cape African voters from the common electoral roll, reflected growing government paranoia about an imagined "threat" to its interests posed by rapidly increasing black migration to urban areas as South Africa began to industrialize. This draconian move radicalized many of the black elite, including Matthews and Jabavu. The latter became president of the All-African Convention, a broad-based ad hoc coalition of black political forces formed in 1935 to protest the Hertzog Acts. The mid-1930s had been a period of profound stagnation in the ANC under its conservative leader Pixley Seme, and so it was the All-African Convention and Jabavu who received great publicity for their principled stand against racial discrimination. Jabavu, who had been educated in Britain and had visited Tuskegee and other African American colleges, had been the first academic appointed to Fort Hare in 1915. At the stage when Mandela got to Fort Hare, however, the All-African Convention was in decline and the ANC, particularly in the Cape Province in which Fort Hare was situated, had begun to revive somewhat under its energetic secretary, the Reverend James Calata, contributing to a subtle but significant general rise of confidence and hope among more politically conscious Africans.

Considering the silences in his autobiography, it is difficult to determine the precise impact these teachers may have had upon Mandela's thinking. Moreover, he was not particularly political in his campus years. Still, it is likely that his teachers' emphasis on African dignity and social equality would have strengthened Mandela's African identity and laid down a bedrock of principled liberalism that later would become an integral part of his political philosophy. The year Mandela arrived at Fort Hare, Matthews and Jabavu had joined forces to lobby government over the low number of black teachers employed; two years later, Jabavu argued in favor of affirmative action for a reduction in the number of non-Africans enrolled at the college in accordance with national demographic ratios.[13]

Despite these more subtle influences from above, there is little evidence of active ANC campaigning at Fort Hare in these days, even though Mandela recalls there were some ANC members among the student body, although he was not one of them. Still rather cautious, he viewed with some concern the radical pronouncements by some ANC-aligned students, such as Nyathi Khongisa, that the government and even the World War Allies were neglecting black interests. Nevertheless, even if he does not seem to have spoken out on national politics or segregation, increasingly Mandela was taking an interest in political events and world affairs. The outbreak of World War II coincided with Mandela's time at Fort Hare, and he enthusiastically applauded an address at the college by Deputy Prime Minister General Jan Smuts, who defended the anti-fascist war effort against opposition by some Afrikaner political parties sympathetic to Germany.

(Afrikaners, a South African white minority (seven percent of the total population, but a majority among whites) speak the Afrikaans language and trace descent from Dutch settlers).

Mandela's initiation into student politics was not long in coming. He was involved in organizing a more representative House Committee for his residence hall, Wesley House. Presently, long-standing student complaints over racial inequality and the poor quality of food served to Africans by the white-run college coincided with his nomination to the Students' Representative Council (SRC). The majority of students, Mandela among them, called for greater SRC powers to address such issues and boycotted the election. When a small number of students did vote, the "elected" councilors refused to sit on the SRC in defiance of Principal Kerr, who exerted strong pressure on the councilors, placing Mandela in a very diffi-cult dilemma; only he stood firm as a matter of principle, refusing to serve. As a result, Mandela's formal education came to an abrupt and unexpected end in November 1940 when Kerr effectively expelled him, directing him to apply for readmission in the New Year if he changed his mind.[14]

Despite this defiance of white authority, Mandela was still hardly an African nationalist activist. Indeed, when during the 1940 winter holi-days, he took home with him a friend, Paul Mahabane—whose father Z. R. Mahabane had served as President-General of the ANC in the 1920s and 1930s—he was aghast when his friend openly refused to serve obedi-ently a local white magistrate who had imperiously ordered him to carry out an errand as if he was a servant. Such arrogance among white South Africans was common at the time, but Mandela's stunned reaction was an indication not only of his then moderate politics and limited contact with such whites in his early years, but also of the numbing effect on black pride of colonialism felt by many Africans.[15]

When Mandela returned, confused, from college at the end of the year to the "Great Place" at Mqhekezweni, the regent, Jongintaba, was furious at his ward's stubborn behavior in opposing the principal's authority. Even more troubling to the young Mandela, Jongintaba announced that his son Justice and Mandela were to be married immediately—both to young women not of their choosing. Justice and Mandela were appalled; more to the point, Mandela's appointed fiancé was in love instead with Justice. To avoid the arranged marriage they decided to run away to the big city of Johannesburg. After illicitly selling two of Jongintaba's cattle, they under-took a dramatic and perilous journey, first by train, during which time the regent's agents almost apprehended them, and finally by car, paying what to them was a considerable sum of money to a white woman to drive them to Johannesburg.

This open challenge to Xhosa kinship authority contrasted with Mandela's then apolitical mood, which was not particularly surprising given his rural background. Although there had been a wave of rural radicalism in the Transkei in the 1920s, this seems to have bypassed the Great Place. Furthermore, the regent, who dutifully attended meetings of the government-funded Transkeian Bhunga, a purely advisory, conservative African council, was hardly a radical influence. Instead, Mandela attributes his social radicalism to his Westernized education, adding, characteristically, that he also "was a romantic, and I was not prepared to have anyone, even the regent, select a bride for me."[16]

Mandela's youth had been a transition to a new, more independent life away from the support of his extended family. He continued to spend his school holidays at home at the Great Place, but generally his mother and sister could not travel the long distance to Fort Hare. In any case, because he had moved to live with the regent, his nuclear family did not keep in touch very much, and the term nuclear family can be misleading in rural African communities where the extended family is very important. Instead, he was looking to the future and making new social contacts.

Throughout his school years, Mandela persevered despite his relative lack of personal resources. The regent did provide for his school expenses as well as some pocket money, but lack of family resources ever since his father had lost the chieftaincy had forced Mandela to rely on others. When he first attended elementary school, he had been obliged to wear his father's hand-me-down clothes that were embarrassingly too large. At Clarkebury, he was the butt of student jokes for the same reason. When he attended Fort Hare, he received his first suit (see photo essay), but there still was a contradiction in the fact that this young man, whom the regent was grooming for service to the Thembu royalty, remained personally quite poor. Mandela threw himself into his studies and until 1941 could rely on the regent's patronage, so his own rather precarious class position did not matter. In years to come, however, his demonstrated sympathy for the plight of ordinary Africans suggests that his more humble background may have blended with his relatively elite education to produce a youth not only well versed in leadership skills but also very sensitive to the position of all Africans suffering under an oppressive social system.

The years of elementary, secondary, and tertiary education at Clarkebury, Healdtown, and Fort Hare had widened the young man's perspectives; they also indicated future challenges. The most significant influences on Mandela during these years were first, the interaction between Western ideas and African indigenous beliefs; second, his grooming as a future Thembu leader; third, his growing sense of identity as both Xhosa and

African; and finally his introduction at Fort Hare to African student and wider nationalist politics. All these influences combined to produce a young man of great sensitivity and self-discipline, prepared to risk his career over a principle, not yet politicized but of a questioning mind. Mandela's abrupt move to the big metropolis of Johannesburg was soon to propel him to the center of African politics and change the entire course of his life.

NOTES

1. Tom Lodge, *Mandela: A Critical Life* (New York: Oxford University Press, 2006), p. 4; Steven Gish, *Alfred B. Xuma: African, American, South African* (New York: New York University Press, 2000), pp. 15–16; "Mandela's Day of Majesty," *Cape Times*, July 12, 1996; Peter Limb, "Early ANC Leaders and the British World: Ambiguities and Identities," *Historia* 47, no. 1 (2002): pp. 56–82.

2. Nelson Mandela, *Long Walk to Freedom: The Autobiography of Nelson Mandela* (Boston: Little, Brown, 1994), pp. 31, 34.

3. *Healdtown 1855–1955: Centenary Brochure* (Healdtown Missionary Institution, 1955); S. M. Molema, *Healdtown 1855–1955: A Scrap of History* (Healdtown, 1955), pp. 5–7.

4. This point is suggested by Tom Lodge in *Mandela: A Critical Life*, p. 5.

5. Mandela, *Long Walk to Freedom*, pp. 33–36; Nelson Mandela interviewed in the film *Mandela: Son of Africa, Father of a Nation*.

6. Office of Chief Magistrate, Transkeian Territories, circulars May 26, 1936, March 19, 1937, Cape Archives Repository, file 1/KNT 40; Mandela, *Long Walk to Freedom*, pp. 33–34, 85.

7. H. L. Henchman, *The Town of Alice with Lovedale and Fort Hare* (Lovedale: Lovedale Press, 1927), pp. 2, 35; Mandela, *Long Walk to Freedom*, p. 37.

8. Mandela, *Long Walk to Freedom*, p. 40; Mary Benson, *Nelson Mandela* (London: Penguin, 1986), pp. 20–21; Martin Meredith, *Nelson Mandela: A Biography* (New York: St. Martin's Press, 1998), pp. 21–22.

9. Nelson Mandela interviewed in 1993, cited in Luli Callinicos, *Oliver Tambo: Beyond the Engeli Mountains* (Cape Town: D. Philip, 2004), pp. 110, 107.

10. "Nelson Mandela," interview with Nadine Gordimer, ca. 1960, in Carter Karis Collection, Center for Research Libraries, Chicago, 2:XM33:91/1.

11. On African interpreters, see Benjamin N. Lawrance, Emily Lynn Osborn, and Richard L. Roberts, eds., *Intermediaries, Interpreters, and Clerks: African Employees in the Making of Colonial Africa* (Madison: University of Wisconsin Press, 2006).

12. Z. K. Matthews, *Freedom for My People: The Autobiography of Z. K. Matthews*, ed. Monica Wilson (Cape Town: David Philip, 1981), chapter 6; Mandela, *Long Walk to Freedom*, p. 38. Mandela's own university records disappeared from Fort Hare some years ago.

13. Catherine Higgs, *The Ghost of Equality: The Public Lives of D. D. T. Jabavu of South Africa, 1885–1959* (Athens: Ohio University Press, 1997), p. 48.

14. Lodge, *Mandela: A Critical Life*, pp. 9–12; Alexander Kerr, *Fort Hare 1915–48: The Evolution of an African College* (New York: Humanities Press, 1968), p. 241. On later student protests at the college see Donovan Williams, *A History of the University College of Fort Hare, South Africa, the 1950s* (Lewiston, NY: E. Mellen Press, 2001).

15. Mandela, *Long Walk to Freedom*, pp. 42–43.

16. Mandela, *Long Walk to Freedom*, p. 47.

Chapter 3

CITY OF GOLD: LAW, MARRIAGE, AND POLITICS

By 1941, when Nelson Mandela reached Johannesburg (known among Africans as Egoli, "City of Gold"), it was the largest and most industrially developed city in South Africa, if not the entire continent of Africa. However, segregation laws marked off the city center and inner neighborhoods as a white city. Mandela and his cousin Justice therefore headed for the gold mines in hope of work and to the black "townships" for a place to live. The next few years were to prove a decisive turning point in his life, but first he had to adapt to life in an entirely different environment.

The city of Johannesburg and surrounding areas, known collectively as the Rand (short for the Witwatersrand, "Ridge of White Water" in Afrikaans), was the site of the fabulously rich gold deposits that since 1886 had driven national economic growth. Yet, although gold had brought great prosperity to white Johannesburg, the lot of black miners was an unhappy one. The gold was deep underground, the work hard and dangerous, with high rates of both industrial accidents and debilitating industrial diseases such as tuberculosis and silicosis. The wages of black miners were pitifully low; effectively they did not change in real terms between 1910 and 1960. Whereas in the United States in this period the gap between white and black wages was narrowing, in South Africa the index of blacks' real earnings actually declined while the corresponding figures for white miners, who earned approximately 15 times more than black miners did, continued to rise. To add to this misery, mine companies and laws strongly discouraged black miners from bringing wives or families with them, forcing them to live in single-sex compounds or hostels where they often slept on crude cement bunks and ate very poor food. Beatings underground from white supervisors were common and often went unchecked. Government and companies opposed African labor unions and it was only in the 1940s that a fragile African Mine Worker's Union was established. The linchpin of these severe industrial relations was the "job color bar" that reserved skilled work for white artisans.[1]

The Johannesburg that Mandela made home was the site of rapid urban change. World War II intensified the pace both of South African industrialization and of black urbanization and incorporation into the work force. Growing pressure to relax segregation and give rights to black unions accompanied these trends. The combination of rigid segregation and mine work had thrown up grim black neighborhoods or "townships," such as the densely populated, chaotic Alexandra to the north of the city and the sprawling settlements to the southwest, later known as Soweto.

Yet despite segregation there were still pockets of multiracial settlement, notably Sophiatown, a neighborhood to the west that sported a vibrant multiculturalism and music. The 1940s also were a time of black literary renaissance. This harsh but vibrant urban world was a novelty for Mandela. He had heard stories of criminal gangs, or tsotsis, on the Rand. He therefore took the precaution of bringing with him a revolver, a measure that proved embarrassing when police charged a friend, conveying for him the weapon, with possession of an unlicensed firearm. Mandela rescued his friend by confessing it was his gun; police released him with a caution.

Justice had an offer of clerical work at Crown Mines and convinced the African works supervisor or induna, Mr. Piliso, to employ Mandela. As a result, in April 1941 Mandela secured temporary work as a security guard at Crown Mines. Within a month, however, the induna discovered the young men's ruse and, angrily waving a telegram from Mandela's guardian the regent Jongintaba that stated, "Send boys home at once," he dismissed them.

The two young men next sought the assistance of a friend of the regent, Alfred Bitini Xuma, one of the very few African medical practitioners on the Rand and, from December 1940, also the President-General of the African National Congress (ANC), the main black political organization. The previous year, following a visit of Jongintaba to his Johannesburg clinic, Xuma had assisted with Mandela's transport to and entrance into Fort Hare,[2] so already there was a relationship between the two men. Xuma's kind offer of assistance to help them find a job on the mines, however, led back only to Mr. Piliso, who again sent the young men packing.

At the age of 23 and with no close kin nearby, Mandela found himself stranded in the bustling city with no job. At first, he obtained temporary

lodgings with a cousin, Garlick Mbekeni, a small trader originally from
Engcobo in Thembuland, who lived in the nearby George Goch Township. A young African nurse who had observed Mandela's poverty-stricken
predicament contacted her friend Albertina Totiwe, who soon helped
Mandela meet her fiancé, Walter Sisulu. The meeting was destined to
change the whole course of Mandela's life.

Like Mandela, Sisulu hailed from Thembuland. Six years Mandela's
elder, he owned one of the few black businesses in Johannesburg, a small
real estate agency called Sitha Investments; Mandela's cousin referred to
Sisulu as "one of our best people in Johannesburg." Despite this apparent success, unlike Mandela, Sisulu was from a modest background—his
Xhosa mother had worked as a domestic servant and his father, a white
assistant magistrate, had abandoned him. As a young man in the 1930s,
Sisulu had labored on the mines and in factories, once losing his job for
leading a strike for a living wage before turning his hand to small business. Sisulu lived in the African dormitory suburb of Orlando, where he
was active in local culture and politics, heading an African choir and
becoming prominent in both a Xhosa cultural body, the Orlando Broth-
erly Association, and the Orlando branch of the ANC. By now city- and
politics-wise, the older man would become Nelson Mandela's mentor.[3]

Arriving at Sisulu's office in downtown Barclay Arcade, the sight of an
African businessperson with his own office and secretary tremendously
impressed Mandela. He was even more amazed to hear that Sisulu lacked a
higher education, but rather had "knowledge and skills from the University
of life." Sisulu, upon hearing that the younger man wished to study law,
detected a future leader of the African community and, only too aware
that he had to deal daily with purely white lawyers, promised to help
secure him a position with a law firm. Years later, Sisulu would recall that
when Mandela first walked into his office, "I knew that he was someone
who would go far and should be encouraged." He could see that Mandela's
"personality was very striking, very warm." The two men soon became
lifelong friends and comrades-in-arms.[4]

In the meantime, in search of a place of his own to stay, Mandela had
moved six miles north of Johannesburg to the black enclave of Alexandra
Township. This was a densely settled square mile that, like Sophiatown,
had somehow survived as a place where Africans could still buy freehold-
title to land—elsewhere they increasingly were pushed into segregated
ghettos. Alexandra, surrounded by affluent white suburbs, was a "black
island in a white sea," yet despite its poverty and jumble of winding
streets—its lack of electricity earned it the nickname "Dark City"—was
a small haven of freedom. It was home to a pulsating black urban culture

that gave birth to such trends as the popular pennywhistle music known as *kwela* jazz (captured in the 1950 film *The Magic Garden*), and to urban self-help associations such as the Daughters of Africa.

To Mandela, "life in Alexandra was exhilarating and precarious"[5] and his personal, working, and political life began to develop. On arrival in Alexandra, he stayed first with the family of the Reverend J. Mabutho, a Thembu and a family friend, but who, after hearing of Mandela's flight from the regent, asked him to leave, although not before assisting him to find a room nearby with the Xhoma family. At that juncture, Mandela fell in love with and courted Ellen Nkabinde, a Swazi woman whom he had known at Healdtown. However, before very long she left town, and they lost touch with each other. Mandela also was attracted to Didi, one of the Xhoma family daughters.

At this time, there was much experimentation among African youth on the Rand with fashion. Cults or gangs known by such names as "Americans" and "Russians" delighted in wearing pin-stripe suits and panama hats and, if they could afford it, drive around in American cars. Mandela, very much drawn to the attractive Didi, felt rather humiliated when, simultaneously, a well-dressed dandy with whom he could not hope to compete in style and expense of clothes courted her. "Didi barely took any notice of me, and what she did notice was the fact that I owned only one patched-up suit . . . [while] her boyfriend wore expensive, double-breasted American suits and wide-brimmed hats."[6]

Despite their poverty, Africans had their music. In the impoverished black townships, music was a vital outlet of expression and could reflect both the frustrations of life and the hope of change. A popular musician of the time, General Duze, who later would play a solidarity benefit concert for the jailed Mandela, recalled that Mandela "liked his jazz" and would jive into the early hours.[7]

Before long, Mandela was offered a job as an articled clerk with Sisulu's client, the law firm of Lazar Sidelsky, Witkin, Sidelsky, and Eidelman. Whereas many whites continued to regard Africans purely as "hewers of wood and drawers of water," Sidelsky, a Jewish lawyer with liberal ideas and in favor of promoting African education, was ahead of his time in encouraging black professionals. He waived Mandela's fee and gave him a loan. Mandela each day took the train to the big city to work in this office located in central Johannesburg. At night, he studied by candlelight to complete his Bachelor of Arts degree by correspondence.

The law firm also employed two other young clerks: Nat Bregman and Gaur Radebe. Both were politically active in the Communist Party of South Africa, at the time the only multiracial political party in the country and which was attracting Africans to its ranks. Radebe also was prominent in the ANC and black labor unions, helping to found the African Mine Workers' Union in 1941, as well as being active in Alexandra bus boycotts. Out of intellectual curiosity and African solidarity, Mandela attended some political meetings and social gatherings, where he met other young radicals, but he did not yet become active in organizations. However, he soaked up ideas on politics, which he viewed chiefly through the lens of racial oppression. When Mandela discovered that blacks and whites by convention had to use separate teacups even in Sidelsky's law office, he realized that racism permeated even many liberal white circles.

Mandela learned about politics not just in Johannesburg. In the 1940s, Alexandra was the site of determined African resistance to white racism and exploitation. To Mandela, Alexandra was not only "a treasured place in my heart," but also a township where Africans of different ethnic backgrounds came together with "a sense of solidarity." In the cold winter of August 1943, Mandela marched with thousands of other protesters in the famous Alexandra bus boycott. Africans refused to accept an imposed price rise they could ill afford and instead walked the 10 miles to work. The long walk was no novelty for Mandela, as his lack of money often meant he had to do the same. After nine days of boycott, the bus company gave in and retracted the fare increases. Even before this, Mandela had begun to meet politically active Africans. Besides Sisulu and Radebe, at the Xhoma's Mandela had met a fellow tenant, Schreiner Baduza, active in the Communist Party. However, it was to the ANC that Mandela would eventually give his loyalty, and Sisulu encouraged him to get involved with the organization.[8]

What helped Mandela make the connection between political theory and practice at this time was his first-hand experience of the harsh conditions of the lives of most urban Africans. In his first year on the Rand, Mandela remained quite poor. He earned only £8 a month, and had to pay £1.5 a month for bus fares and nearly the same again for rent, as well as paying university fees. Once he bought basic foodstuffs, and candles to study by, there was precious little left for things like clothes. Therefore, Mandela was most grateful to his landlord Mr. Xhoma for the regular hearty Sunday dinner he offered free of charge.

Alexandra was terribly overcrowded and there were frequent police raids to arrest Africans who lacked or may have simply mislaid their "passes." To Africans the pass laws were the supreme symbol of segregation (and later of apartheid): without a stamped passbook, an African could be "endorsed out" of the cities that whites regarded as their own

preserve. Police jailed thousands upon thousands of Africans of different income levels over minor pass law infringements, with some of them
sent to work on prison farms. Police also frequently arrested or accosted
African women for brewing traditional African beer, and this treatment
of women was another cause of intense resentment.

In 1942, after living for one year in Alexandra, Mandela moved in
for a short time with a Thembu clansman at the Witwatersrand Native
Labour Association compound, where he had free accommodation. Here
he met African royals visiting their clansmen working on the mines; one
such royal acquaintance was the Queen Regent of Basutoland, who gently
chided Mandela for his inability to speak other African languages besides
isiXhosa, his own language. Around this time, he also met and was reconciled with the regent, then visiting Johannesburg. Sadly, it was the last
time Mandela was to see him alive, as Jongintaba died in mid-1942.

Justice and Mandela hurried home to Mqhekezweni but were just too
late for the funeral. Even though he lingered a week at the Great Place,
Mandela's outlook on life had changed: unlike Justice, who remained
to succeed his father as Paramount Chief, Mandela returned to Johannesburg determined to follow his own calling. In December of 1942, he
finally earned the coveted Bachelor of Arts degree and the following
month attended the graduation ceremony at Fort Hare. Members of his
family including his mother and sister attended, but although the reconciliation with the regent had helped restore his faith in his Thembu culture, and despite being encouraged by his kinsman Kaiser Matanzima to
return to the Transkei to practice law, Mandela was now independent of
the Thembu royal family.

Inspired by the commitment and politics of activists such as Sisulu and
Radebe to a broad, inclusive African nationalism, Mandela felt "all the
currents in my life were taking me away from the Transkei and towards
what seemed like the center, a place where regional and ethnic loyalties
gave way before a common purpose." Thinking at his graduation about
how much things had changed since he had first gone to Fort Hare, Mandela mused that "Having a successful career and comfortable salary were
no longer my ultimate goals. I found myself being drawn into the world of
politics because I was not content with my old beliefs."[9]

The year 1942 witnessed an even more significant event: Mandela, at
the urging of Sisulu and Radebe, made contact with the ANC, the oldest
African political organization in the country. Africans from all around the
country had founded the ANC in 1912 in response to the 1910 Union of
South Africa, which had instituted a whites-only government. For three
decades, the ANC (or "Congress" as it was widely known) had patiently

pursued a policy of peaceful and polite petitions that the all-white government invariably had ignored. At times Congress had campaigned vigorously against discriminatory legislation such as the 1913 Natives' Land Act and passes, but the 1930s had seen its own fortunes decline. However, under the leadership of the Johannesburg-based A. B. Xuma (ANC president 1940–1949), the movement not only revived but also modernized.

Xuma, espousing African nationalist and liberal philosophies, had studied and worked in the United States for 13 years before returning to South Africa to work as one of the very few black physicians. He oversaw the ANC's steady growth to a more centralized, financially viable body. Membership grew from a mere 1,000 in the 1930s to 5,500 by 1947. Xuma's reforms included equality of membership for women, confirmed in a new 1943 ANC constitution and the 1948 refounding of the ANC Women's League, improvements encouraged by Xuma's African American second wife, Madie Hall. Inspired by the Atlantic Charter of the Allies in World War II, Xuma established a committee that coauthored *Africans' Claims in South Africa* (1943), a document calling for African self-determination. He also forged an alliance with the South African Indian Congress and strengthened ties with African labor unions.[10]

These changes in African politics resonated across the country as World War II intensified the entire political scene in South Africa. Some extreme Afrikaner nationalists, traditionally opposed to Britain and influenced by ideas of racial supremacy, supported the rise of Nazism and Fascism in Europe, and their Brownshirt, Greyshirt, and Blackshirt gangs directed hate campaigns against both Africans and Jews in 1940s Johannesburg. Combined with the thousand small jibes and insults of a racist society, Mandela began to move inexorably toward politicization. "I had no epiphany, no singular revelation, no moment of truth, but a steady accumulation of a thousand slights, a thousand indignities . . . produced in me an anger, a rebelliousness, a desire to fight the system that imprisoned my people."[11]

The 1940s were a time of revival for African politics, in Johannesburg in particular. This political revival reflected socioeconomic conditions, changes, and the influence of new ideas. Despite the emergence of a pulsating African urban culture in this decade, facilities for the black middle class were scanty: the few football (soccer) fields that existed for blacks were bare and sandy, there were few African cinemas, and segregation and condescension were everywhere. Working and living conditions for the majority of Africans were bad. At the same time, the war years and particularly U.S. President Franklin D. Roosevelt's intervention in the Atlantic Charter raised the possibility of eventual African decolonization, and this aroused broad feelings of African nationalism, especially among idealistic young people such as Mandela.

Interest in politics signaled Mandela's decisive move away from a narrow Xhosa outlook toward an inclusive African nationalism that has always been the hallmark of "Congress." At first, however, Mandela played a low-key role in African politics. He was still very busy with his education. In early 1943, after completing his law articles, he enrolled in a part-time law degree program at the University of the Witwatersrand (commonly known as "Wits"), a leading university of the country. Despite an undercurrent of racism among some whites at the university—one of Mandela's law professors openly declared that women and blacks were "biologically" ill-suited to becoming lawyers, and blacks were excluded from university sports facilities and residences—Wits was, by South African standards of the time, a liberal university. Unlike Afrikaner universities, Wits at least allowed a small number of black students to enroll. Still, Mandela was the only African student in the entire Law Faculty.

Far from shielding Mandela from politics, the Wits experience opened new contacts. For the first time, he now met and befriended progressive, politicized whites of his own age such as Joe Slovo and radical Indian South African law students such as J. N. Singh and Ismail Meer. Singh, Meer, and Slovo were all members of the Communist Party. The friends spent many nights discussing politics and socializing at Meer's inner-city apartment, which Mandela found a convenient retreat to avoid evening curfews imposed on Africans. But in many ways he was the odd-man-out.

Although impressed by some of the tenets of Marxism such as the classless society, Mandela hotly opposed communism in favor of African nationalism. Nevertheless, he began to appreciate that his new white and Indian friends were fully prepared to support the gathering national liberation struggle of Africans; in Mandela's words, they were prepared "to sacrifice themselves for the cause of the oppressed." On one occasion Meer, Singh, and Mandela, alighting without realizing it on a segregated tram, objected to the subsequent unconcealed racism of the conductor and found themselves arrested. The next day the court exonerated the young men when their lawyer, another progressively minded friend and part-time lecturer Bram Fischer, whose father was the Judge-President of the Orange Free State, impressed the magistrate.[12]

Besides his studies, another factor initially inclining Mandela away from involvement in full-time politics was his growing family commitment. In 1944, he met Evelyn Mase, a cousin of Walter Sisulu and, like Sisulu, also from Engcobo in Thembuland. The couple had met in the crowded home of Sisulu and his wife Albertina, where at times Mandela stayed. Almost at once Mandela fell in love with Evelyn. It was the same with her; "I loved him the first time I saw him . . . there was something very special about Nelson." The couple married a month later in a quiet civil ceremony in Johannesburg. They lacked enough money for a traditional wedding and feast and were similarly obliged by lack of finance and the dearth of black housing to live first with Evelyn's brother in Orlando East and then with her sister and husband in a small house at City Deep Mines. Later, in 1947, they moved into a tiny three-roomed "matchbox" house, not far from the Sisulus in the barren landscape collectively known as Soweto, where the government had decided to dump Africans.[13]

Their first son, Madiba Thembekile (Thembi), was born in 1946. Mandela "delighted in playing with Thembi, bathing him and feeding him, and putting him to bed with a little story." He enjoyed domesticity, and Evelyn later reminisced that he also enjoyed doing the family shopping, even on occasions taking "over the cooking from us women." He was, she notes, a well-organized person who rose at dawn, went jogging, and had a light breakfast, but politics increasingly kept him very busy. "I was rarely at home to enjoy these things," he later wrote. Evelyn had company when first Mandela's sister Leabie joined them from the countryside to attend school, and then later his mother visited. There often were other visitors from the Transkei. A daughter, Makaziwe, was born in 1948 but was very frail. She died after only nine months, to the great distress of her parents.[14]

Evelyn Mase, born in 1922, was very different in personality than Mandela. Devoutly religious and rather apolitical, she did not share his enthusiasm for politics, although for a period she was encouraged by Oliver Tambo's wife Adelaide to become active in the nurses' labor union. In contrast to the noble-born Mandela, her father was a humble mineworker, and both her parents died when she was a child. When they first met, she was training to be a nurse. Evelyn supported Mandela, still studying, by working for a year in what she later described as a "terrible" job with a mining company that paid the tiny amount of only seven and a half pounds a month.[15]

By 1944, Mandela had established himself in Johannesburg. He had got used to the fast pace of urban living, completed his Bachelor of Arts, embarked on professional legal studies, and started a family. Yet despite the obligations of marriage and the rigor of legal studies, the political ideas and experiences that Mandela had piece by piece imbued over the last few years now began to crystallize around the need he perceived to actually do something about the awful predicament of his people.

Nelson Mandela was about to launch himself into the maelstrom of African politics that, over the next decade, would see him rise rapidly to become a prominent African political leader and a household name across the country. He was to do this initially through an energetic new youth organization allied to the ANC that he would help develop with the support of friends such as Sisulu and Oliver Tambo, his old student friend from Fort Hare.

NOTES

1. Francis Wilson, *Labour in the South African Gold Mines 1911–1969* (Cambridge: Cambridge University Press, 1972), chapter 3.

2. Steven Gish, *Alfred B. Xuma: African, American, South African* (New York: New York University Press, 2000), p. 253.

3. Nelson Mandela, *Long Walk to Freedom: The Autobiography of Nelson Mandela* (Boston: Little, Brown, 1994), pp. 59–60.

4. Elinor Sisulu, *Walter and Albertina Sisulu: In Our Lifetime* (Cape Town: D. Philip, 2002), pp. 64–65; Walter Sisulu, *I Will Go Singing: Walter Sisulu Speaks of His Life and the Struggle for Freedom in South Africa* (Cape Town: Robben Island Museum, 2001), p. 40.

5. Mandela, *Long Walk to Freedom*, p. 66.

6. Mandela, *Long Walk to Freedom*, p. 70.

7. Gwen Ansell, *Soweto Blues: Jazz, Popular Music and Politics in South Africa* (New York: Continuum, 2004), p. 115.

8. Mandela, *Long Walk to Freedom*, p. 67; Tom Lodge, *Mandela: A Critical Life* (New York: Oxford University Press, 2006), p. 23.

9. Mandela, *Long Walk to Freedom*, pp. 72–73.

10. Gish, *Alfred B. Xuma*; Peter Walshe, *The Rise of African Nationalism in South Africa: The African National Congress, 1912–1952* (Berkeley: University of California Press, 1971).

11. Interview with Colin Tatz by the author, Sydney, Australia, August 9, 2005; Mandela, *Long Walk to Freedom*, p. 83.

12. Mandela, *Long Walk to Freedom*, pp. 79–80; Ismail Meer, *A Fortunate Man* (Cape Town: Zebra Press, 2002), pp. 81–82.

13. Mandela, *Long Walk to Freedom*, pp. 88–92; Meer, *Higher than Hope*, pp. 39–41.

14. Mandela, *Long Walk to Freedom*, pp. 88–92; Meer, *Higher than Hope*, pp. 39–41.

15. Evelyn Mase and Anthony Sampson, interviewed in the documentary film *Mandela: Son of Africa, Father of a Nation*.

Chapter 4

POLITICS: YOUTH LEAGUE AND THE AFRICAN NATIONAL CONGRESS

The bubbling cauldron of African politics in the 1940s produced a new youth organization that reinvigorated black opposition to the harsh policies of segregation and exploitation. Nelson Mandela increasingly moved to the center of this new African politics that was strident, assertive, and impatient with the established, moderate *hamba kahle* (literally "go well" in Zulu, but here meaning "softly, softly" or indecisive) ANC "Old Guard" leadership. When in 1948 white politics lurched sharply to the right with the election by the all-white electorate of the National Party, the stage was set for a major confrontation drawn on both political and racial lines in which Mandela would be center-stage.

A complex situation now developed within the ANC. Xuma wanted to build the organization into an effective machine. When a rival body, the African Democratic Party, emerged in September 1943, Xuma increased his wooing of the youth to try to recruit new members and keep the ANC from splitting. In the same year, he had introduced a reformed ANC constitution, also indicative of his drive to expand and modernize the ANC.

At the same time, a deep rivalry was brewing between on the one hand Xuma and the "Old Guard" and, on the other hand, young radicals such as Mandela. Ironically, Xuma actually encouraged the youth to take a greater role. For example, he asked them to draft various policy documents and letters. He also enjoyed meeting with the youth at his home, called "Empilweni," in Sophiatown, a neighborhood a few miles from central Johannesburg. In the face of the challenge posed by the African Democratic Party, it seems likely that Xuma favored incorporating youthful dissent *within* the ANC. Hence, he had supported a successful motion

at the ANC's national conference in December 1943 calling for the establishment of a youth wing, but on the understanding that this was to help
recruitment to the ANC.

Mandela, Sisulu, and others recognized the importance of the ANC
as the major African political organization capable of actually achieving
civil rights and freedom for Africans. Indeed, in their first policy statement the young radicals conceded that a youth organization, while serving to coordinate "all youthful forces employed in rousing popular political
consciousness and fighting oppression and reaction," must also "not be
allowed to detract Youth's attention" from the ANC. However, they were
concerned that its pace of change was too slow to be effective in the
face of ever-hardening anti-African attitudes by the government. Moreover, whereas Xuma viewed the youth as merely a wing of the more senior
ANC, young activists such as Mandela wanted more autonomy, and they
wanted militant ANC policies. Writing 50 years later, Mandela mused
that young Africans of the time "felt, perhaps unfairly, that the ANC as a
whole had become the preserve of a tired, unmilitant, privileged African
elite more concerned with protecting their own rights than those of the
masses." Although he acknowledged the profound work Xuma was doing
for Africans, Mandela could not help but notice Xuma's "air of supercil-
iousness that did not befit the leader of a mass organization. As devoted as
he was to the ANC, his medical practice took precedence. . . . Everything
was done in the English manner, the idea being that despite our disagreements we were all gentlemen."[1]

Matters came to a head when the young radicals drafted a manifesto
highly critical of the Old Guard for its failure effectively to combat white
domination. In 1943, they met with Xuma to discuss their concerns.
Mandela recalls that the rather "paternalistic" ANC President-General
bluntly told them he opposed a separate Youth League with a separate
constitution and that their call for mass campaigns was premature and
dangerous. On February 21, 1944, Sisulu, Mandela, and two other young
activists, J. Congress Mbata and William Nkomo, met again with Xuma
in Sophiatown, but he remained obdurate. As a result, on Easter Sunday, in April of 1944, at a meeting of some one hundred people at the
Bantu Men's Social Center in Johannesburg, they provisionally founded
the Congress Youth League (later ANC Youth League). Mandela was a
founding member.[2]

In this period, Mandela had greatly widened his circle of political comrades. In 1943, he had joined the loosely based "Graduates" discussion
group among young educated Africans in Johannesburg. He made contact
again and began a close friendship with his acquaintance from Fort Hare

college days, Oliver Tambo, who had moved back to the city to teach science at St. Peters school after completing his studies. The British journalist Anthony Sampson, a close friend of Mandela, describes the partnership between the two men as crucial to African politics, with Tambo more reflective, the deep thinker, and Mandela more the militant activist leader, with his commanding physique.[3]

Mandela continued to learn about politics from mentors such as Walter Sisulu. It was at Sisulu's house in Orlando, Soweto, that Mandela in 1943 met two youth activists, Anton Muziwakhe Lembede and A. P. Mda. The brilliant young lawyer Lembede, together with the cerebral Mda and Tambo, would provide much of the initial intellectual drive for the formation of the Congress Youth League.

The original philosophy of Lembede epitomized the assertive Africanism of the Youth League. Coming from a poor peasant background in KwaZulu-Natal province, he had risen rapidly in black political circles after completing Master of Arts and Bachelor of Law degrees and then joining the legal firm of Pixley Seme, an ANC founder. Lembede articulated a clear vision of an assertive Africanism, or Black Nationalism, that cast off any pretence of the need for paternalistic white guidance, instead calling for African self-reliance and self-determination. The March 1944 Manifesto of the provisional Congress Youth League asserted these views, stating, "Africans must struggle for development, progress and national liberation so as to occupy their rightful and honorable place among nations of the world." The League absorbed most ANC policies, from full civil rights for Africans to support for black labor unions but made clear that the Youth League was to be the "brains-trust and power-station of the spirit of African nationalism."[4]

From the outset, Lembede deeply impressed Mandela, who later characterized him as "a magnetic personality who thought in original and often startling ways." To Mandela, the Youth League Manifesto represented the explanation and codification of African nationalism. On the other hand, as Mandela's lifelong friend Tambo commented in 1973, in "the many long meetings held between Lembede, Mda, Sisulu, Mandela and myself, Mandela was not one with Lembede on those positions which could be described as ultra-nationalistic." Mandela's later acceptance of ANC unity with other political organizations, including those of progressive white and Indian South Africans, reflected his more broad-minded approach to African nationalism.[5]

The Congress Youth League at first had a provisional structure, and at its inaugural gathering at Easter 1944 elected Mandela to the Executive Committee. Its first official public conference took place in September

1944, heralded by a flyer entitled *Trumpet Call to Youth*. Henceforth, it became a major force in ANC politics. Membership was open to all African males and females between the ages of 12 and 40, and those members over 17 years of age automatically also became ANC members. The main office-holders were Lembede (president), Tambo (secretary), and Sisulu (treasurer). Mandela was not yet an office holder in the organization, but he was a member of the executive committee and his presence in the high-level delegations to visit Xuma indicates that already he was regarded as a "shaker and mover" within its ranks.[6]

The extent to which Mandela was involved in the actual formulation and drafting of these seminal Youth League policy statements is not clear, although he appears to have had an input into its Manifesto and Basic Policy document. However, the major political thinkers at this stage were Lembede and Tambo, with Mandela and Sisulu best typified as action-oriented. In this period, Mandela was not yet prominent in internal debates or in public pronouncements. He was not, for example, a speaker at the first major public meeting of the Youth League in September 1944, and he was not recorded as a speaker at the decisive December 1949 conference of the ANC that saw the triumph of the Youth League's Program of Action.

Amidst all this political ferment, Mandela was getting married, raising a family, working in the daytime as a legal clerk, and studying at night for a law degree. Therefore, it is a tribute to his characteristic energy and commitment, and the support of his wife and friends, that he was able to play such a central role in events of such importance.

Mandela's daily routine reflected his limited income: for transport, he was reliant on buses and trains and he ate sparingly. From an early age, Mandela was a teetotaler, and his youthful athleticism continued, with boxing workouts becoming a favorite method of relaxation and exercise. In 1947, through this interest he met the boxing champion of Soweto, Jerry Moloi. Tall and handsome, Mandela's athletic appearance exuded youthful vitality and strength that is well captured in a contemporary photograph of him boxing (see photographic essay).

Despite all his political activity, Mandela continued his law studies. In 1948, he gained the coveted position of an articled law clerk, but in December 1949, with much of his time taken up elsewhere in escalating political duties, he failed his university law examinations. It would take him another three years, this time studying within the legal profession, finally to complete his credentialing as an attorney.

Family life also had to take a back seat to politics. In 1946, the Mandelas moved into their own simple home in Orlando East. The house, designated

"Orlando 8115," was a tiny two-bedroom box, in Mandela's words "built on postage-stamp-size plots on dirt roads. It had the same standard tin roof, the same cement floor, a narrow kitchen, and bucket toilet." Kerosene lamps served for lighting, as the white authorities denied Africans electricity—only in the 1990s were many houses eventually connected.

A neighbor, Es'kia Mphahlele, (later a famous writer) wrote of the "squalor and poverty" and that "the only beautiful thing about Orlando was the street lights looked at across from our dark west end of the township." After a short time, the Mandelas moved to a slightly larger house in Orlando West. Evelyn Mandela was very supportive (Mandela remembered her as a "quiet lady, devoted to her family and husband"), but does not seem to have shown any interest in politics, seeing him, she later recalled, not as a politician but as a student. Mandela's sister Leabie, who lived with them for a time, observed that Evelyn "didn't want to hear a thing about politics."[7] His greatly increasing political duties therefore were bound eventually to strain their relations. In the meantime, however, family life proceeded happily. In 1949, Mandela's mother, who was unwell, came to stay and got on well with his wife.

As discussed in the previous chapter, the years of World War II brought new energy and optimism to African political circles. However, even though Africans strongly supported the Allied cause, there was lingering resentment at the government's failure to arm Africans and especially at the fact that, following a war fought against fascism and racism, the government, instead of abolishing segregation, as it had hinted at during the war years, now moved to step up repression. The war years had seen a temporary halt to vigorous demands for black rights, but the government exploited this to crack down on black labor unions and intensify the implementation of pass laws. This attempt by South Africa's white rulers to turn the clock back was swimming against the tide of history. The world was changing. There was considerable interest among Africans in the way in which Japan was able to defeat a European power, the British army, in Southeast Asia and in the growing independence movement in India and other countries.

Against this backdrop, the material conditions of the overwhelming majority of black people had deteriorated. War rationing and rising inflation hit their ranks hardest. Accelerating urban migration during the war years saw a sharp increase in the black workforce—more than 100,000 new jobs for Africans were created, many in semiskilled positions previously held by whites, while the number of Africans in Johannesburg grew from 229,000 in 1936 to 371,000 in 1946. During the war years there was significant structural economic change; the number of Africans in manufacturing increased by 57 percent. The war years also saw frequent food shortages. There was a rise in the disease rate among mineworkers related to food shortages on the Rand in the 1940s, and lack of protective equipment for African miners saw increasing rates of industrial accidents. Conditions were no better in the black townships, where infant mortality and poverty-related diseases were rife.

There was an equally sharp decline in the supply and quality of housing for those destitute Africans forced to live in makeshift squatter camps. Housing shortages were particularly acute, with a census counting 2,107 black families squatting in Orlando, not far from where Mandela lived. Here the colorful and enigmatic James "Sofasonke" ("We Shall Die") Mpanza, housed in a tent and often seen riding a horse, emerged as a leader of a squatting movement that mobilized some 70,000 Africans. The Old Guard ANC leadership had great difficulty linking up with this diffuse movement, but Mandela, having experienced life in squalid urban conditions when he first moved to the Rand, felt empathy. He provided free legal advice to the unpredictable and anarchistic Mpanza, evidence of Mandela's generosity and willingness to assist his fellow Africans. And yet, in the years from 1944 to 1946 the main impetus for mass action for change came not from Mandela and the Congress Youth League, but from other directions.

In the 1940s, with the white government increasingly unwilling to listen to African petitions, the ANC under Xuma began cautiously to explore the possibilities for political alliances with other organizations opposed to segregation and supportive of black rights. These alternatives comprised other African organizations, labor unions, multiracial political parties, and Indian and Colored (Creole) organizations.

White political parties generally remained hostile to black membership, and many black people resented the paternalism of white liberals, a feeling that intensified with the rise of African nationalism. However, united action was possible between the ANC and labor unions, some of which represented black workers or still had overlapping black and white membership. Xuma built bridges to the newly formed African Mine Workers Union and Council of Non-European Trade Unions. He spoke out in favor of legalizing black labor unions and supported better conditions and wages for the poorly paid black mineworkers.

Mandela witnessed a major strike by some 70,000 black mineworkers that erupted on the gold mines between August 12 and 16, 1946. Between 1914 and 1941, African mine wages had risen only 1/1d (about a dime) per week, compared to raises 10 to 20 times more in other sectors. There was no provision for leave, no sick pay, and miners complained of inadequate and deteriorating food. Starting work at 3 A.M., they received only *mbunyane intlokoyekati* ("small as a cat's head") bread, were not given time off for lunch, and in the evening were fed thin porridge they called *lambalazi* ("water that makes you hungry"). Raw meat of poor quality was given only about three times a week; with nowhere to keep the meat, it sometimes rotted. Mine compounds were overcrowded, with rooms about 25 feet times 25 feet housing 40 to 80 men. A state commission in 1943 heard evidence of management's use of dogs and thick rhino-hide whips (*sjamboks*). Vermin, bad sewerage, and inadequate coal for heating completed a damning indictment of facilities. The government ruthlessly suppressed the 1946 industrial action by military means, killing 12 miners and wounding 324, effectively destroying the African Mine Workers Union, which did not reemerge for 40 years.[8]

The strike received firm support from the ANC and the Youth League. In a flyer, the Youth League declared strong solidarity with the strikers, stating that the "Mine Workers' struggle is our struggle. . . . We demand a living wage for all African workers!!!!" However, these verbal expressions of solidarity were largely ineffective; the ANC and Youth League lacked their own press to publicize their views, and ANC President Xuma was unwilling to call a general strike in sympathy. These momentous events deeply moved Mandela and drove him toward action. Some of his relatives worked on the mines. He later wrote that during the strike, "I visited them, discussed the issues, and expressed my support" for their struggles. Mandela also went from mine to mine with the leader of the African Mine Workers Union, J. B. Marks, "talking to workers and planning strategy." Marks was a leading figure in both the Transvaal ANC and the Communist Party, and it was characteristic of Mandela's propensity to cooperate (and of the dire situation that blacks found themselves in, requiring the widest possible alliances) that he was willing to work with all those prepared to work for the rights of Africans. The close-knit organization and control over membership of the union, which must have contrasted vividly with what he knew of the more meandering Congress and Youth League bodies, also impressed Mandela.[9]

Another possibility of united action for the ANC lay with the Communist Party of South Africa (CPSA). Originally a largely white party, by the late 1920s it had embraced multiracial membership and soon two-thirds of the organization was black. In the 1930s, it had suffered serious decline due to sectarian policies, but by the 1940s it was more active and attentive to questions of African national liberation. Yet if CPSA leadership included some blacks, such as Moses Kotane and J. B. Marks, also active in the ANC, then much of its leadership remained in white hands. Therefore Mandela, who favored African nationalism over communism,

gained the impression of a white-led party. In this period, Mandela and
Tambo constantly sought to out-maneuver communist candidates for
election to the Transvaal provincial organization of the ANC. On the
other hand, Xuma as ANC leader, if sharing this suspicion of the communists, was more amenable to united action. In this regard, the hard work
undertaken for the ANC by African communists such as Kotane, who
seemed to put African nationalism first, impressed Xuma—and the young
Mandela—but both men remained unconvinced by CPSA ideology and
thoroughly committed to African nationalism.

In the 1940s, the ANC also began seriously to discuss the possibilities of
alliances with political organizations of South African Indians. Historically,
there had been some tension between Africans and Indians. The British
had brought Indian indentured laborers to Natal from the 1860s to the early
twentieth century. Indian traders, who soon aroused the ire of Africans as
a more privileged intermediary social stratum dominating the retail trade,
accompanied the laborers. Imperial Britain and then the white Union of
South Africa were able to "divide and rule" by granting Indian and Colored
communities limited civil rights, which were denied to Africans.

Out of this fractious history, certain widely held and unfortunate ethnic
stereotypes emerged. One of these was the fallacious notion that Indian
South Africans comprised essentially an exploitative caste. In the opinion
of his Indian friend Ismail Meer, Mandela too at this time was inclined to
this view when it came to collective political discussions. However, if in
public Mandela continued to stand aloof from organized cooperation with
whites or Indians, then his sense of fair play and his outgoing and friendly
character would help him triumph over the intolerance fostered by a harsh
divide and rule policy. In Meer's words, the two friends' "personal friendship and trust overcame prejudice and distrust, and paved the way for
united action." At the same time, escalating repression by the government
was pushing different organizations and individuals closer together. The
growing spirit of cooperation is captured by Mary Benson (soon to befriend
Mandela), who writes of how, in Meer's central Johannesburg apartment,
"over endless cups of tea and curry meals at any time of the day or night,"
Mandela and his Indian friends "discussed and argued and planned, they
studied and they listened to the gramophone." Mandela also began to
admire the actions and writings of Jawaharlal Nehru, who in August 1947
led India to independence from Britain.[10] If ideologically Mandela stuck
rigidly to the Youth League policy of "go it alone," then socially he effortlessly sliced through the artificial racial barriers of a rigid society.

Harsh anti-Indian legislation (the 1943 "Pegging" Act and the 1946
Asiatic Land Tenure Act) that restricted their property rights in 1946

provoked a well-organized Passive Resistance Campaign launched by the Transvaal Indian Congress and the Natal Indian Congress. Their model of action was along the lines of the civil disobedience protests initiated three decades earlier by Mahatma Gandhi, during his South African years. The 1946 protests were widespread and marked by great self-discipline: groups of 20 people at a time set up tents on "white" land, courting arrest. Mandela did not fail to notice their determination and discipline; 2,000 were jailed, with the leaders sentenced to six months hard labor merely for defending their right to own property. Friends of his such as Ismail Meer and J. N. Singh put aside their studies to protest. Amina Pahad, with whom Mandela often lunched, went to jail for protesting. He became convinced of the commitment of Indian people to fighting oppression, and their protests became a model for future ANC campaigns; it "broke the fear of prison."[11]

As a result, for the first time representatives of the government of India, working in tandem with South African Indian leaders, placed racism in South Africa on the agenda of the newly formed United Nations (UN). Xuma, representing the ANC, joined in the protests, attending the first session of the UN.

Out of these protests arose the idea for better-coordinated action among all those opposing segregation. The ANC and the Indian Congresses agreed on a "Votes for All" campaign. In 1947, the ANC and Indian Congress leaders Yusuf Dadoo and Monty Naicker signed a joint agreement for closer political cooperation, known as the Xuma-Dadoo-Naicker (or "Doctors") Pact. One of the nerve centers planning the protests was the apartment of Ismail Meer. However, Mandela and the Youth League disapproved of the move, claiming Africans had not initiated it. Although Mandela had initially agreed to work for the Votes for All campaign and had even chaired a meeting, he now withdrew. At this time, he and the Youth League therefore tended to remain aloof from these unity moves and to oppose united action with other organizations unless the ANC or Youth League initiated campaigns.[12]

Tensions between Africans and Indians erupted in serious riots in January 1949 in Durban, occasioned by a chance incident, but in part incubated by the "divide and rule" policies of the white authorities. When the ANC and Natal Indian Congress established a joint council to overcome such conflict, Tambo was involved for the Youth League, which, however, disapproved of the move, claiming it was ineffective. Nonetheless, the Youth League and Mandela gradually tempered their extreme nationalism. In 1948, the League conceded that the system of white domination also oppressed Indians and that all national groups had a right to stay in

South Africa. It seems that Tambo and Sisulu, who already held a broader view of African nationalism, were instrumental in this shift. Mandela remained skeptical of joint action.[13]

The point here is that Mandela did not express racist, anti-Indian prejudices—indeed he had acquired Indian friends since his student days—but rather he insisted, following Lembede, on the need for Africans to make their own decisions and to lead as the indigenous people and the overwhelming majority of the country.

The late 1940s saw a heady contest of ideologies. Mandela and his colleagues vigorously debated the respective merits of African nationalism, communism, civil disobedience, strikes, and direct action. This was a time of flux, of experimentation with new ideas and tactics, and adaptation. By 1950, Mandela remained thoroughly committed to African nationalism as his core set of beliefs, but the determined protests of both Indians and communists made him rethink his earlier exclusionist approach. If in these debates Mandela displayed his characteristic stubbornness and firm adherence to principle, he also was flexible enough to learn the lessons of these political battles.

By now, Mandela's political activities were not restricted to the Youth League. He increasingly identified with the ANC mother body. Although his original Congress membership cards remain lost, Mandela formally joined the ANC in April 1944—it was automatic upon joining the Youth League.[14] In 1947, ANC delegates elected Mandela to the Executive Council of the movement's Transvaal provincial branch.

In the same year, the brilliant Youth League president, Lembede, died at the young age of only 33; Mandela had met with him shortly before his death.[15] At first, the League's strength had been in the Transvaal province, but by 1948 it extended its influence to other regions of the country. Mandela became the League's general secretary, and the tempo of his political life intensified. Now he was responsible for the day-to-day administration and the expansion of the League nationwide. In this, he had considerable success, and the League developed active branches, including at Mandela's alma mater, Fort Hare. Due in no small part to his organizing efforts, reputation, contacts, and popularity within the League, the wider ANC and even its allied organizations grew, forming the basis for his launch into ANC politics the following year.

The Youth League under Mandela's stewardship also grew substantially in stature and size. Soon it was poised to contest the ANC elections. At the same time, dramatic events in the white electorate were to provide African political leaders such as Mandela with unforeseen opportunities to build a mass movement for black civil rights.

The May 26, 1948 election was a watershed in South African history. Contested essentially by whites-only, victory went by a narrow margin to the National Party with its central policy of intensified racial separation and oppression, colloquially termed *apartheid* ("apartness" or separation in the Afrikaans language). The National Party, a more extreme wing of white politics, represented conservative Afrikaners, based especially among farmers but also representing urban intellectuals and employees and the growing power of Afrikaner financial institutions. The full imposition of apartheid would take many years and involve legalized racial discrimination unique in world history and with it massive social engineering—including the forced relocation of millions of Africans—not seen in the world since the days of Hitler. Mandela termed it an "insane policy."

The introduction of apartheid marked a fundamental deterioration in the position of black people across South Africa. To explain why the country lurched from a variety of racial segregation in some ways similar to that found in the American South at this time to the even more extreme form of apartheid, it is necessary to understand its origins.

The genesis of the policy of apartheid goes back to the rising influence of Afrikaner nationalism in the 1930s. Historically, Afrikaner rule in the nineteenth century Republics of the Transvaal and Orange Free State had legally subordinated Africans, excluding them from both church and state. In the twentieth century, Afrikaners continued to comprise a numerical majority of the electorate, which remained essentially white, with very few blacks allowed to vote. Resentment among Afrikaners of English-speaking white South Africans continued to build after the South African ("Boer") War of 1899–1902. This took the form of an Afrikaner cultural revivalism around the Afrikaans language. Rising Afrikaner nationalism also manifested in early political pressure groups such as the Broederbond ("brotherhood," founded in 1918), a secret society that would exert considerable influence on apartheid policy-makers.[16]

A rise in Afrikaner political conservatism and cultural nationalism, backed by a Calvinist-inspired manifest destiny notion that somehow they must be the "chosen people" of God marked the 1930s. In 1934, the Purified National Party (later National Party) under D. F. Malan broke away from relatively moderate Afrikaner political forces. In the same year, Afrikaner politicians and intellectuals mobilized around the centenary of the Great Trek and the related building of the Voortrekker Monument to white victories over Africans in frontier wars.

National Party leaders D. F. Malan and Hendrik Verwoerd were the architects of apartheid. Malan had used the term "apartheid" from the 1930s as he distanced his party from British traditions of liberalism and even from the policy of segregation, which he saw as too "lenient" on blacks. During World War II, some National Party leaders even went as far as identifying with Nazi Germany. Verwoerd, educated in pre-Nazi Germany, was the ideologue of apartheid. He became Native Affairs Minister in the early 1950s and later Prime Minister.[17]

There also was an economic angle to the origins of apartheid. At this time, Afrikaner capital resources expanded in corporations such as the insurance company Sanlam, reflecting rising Afrikaner economic power that felt marginalized by big British capital grouped in the banks and in mining houses such as the Anglo-American and De Beers companies.

In an attempt to win political power and consolidate their economic interests, extremist Afrikaner politicians turned to the "race card" to whip up white electoral support. Rapid mechanization during World War II heightened competition for jobs, stimulating a racist reaction among some white employees concerned about the apparent erosion of segregation. Apartheid's impact on the economy would be complex. In some ways, it definitely benefited the capitalist system by guaranteeing a steady flow of cheap black labor to companies; on the other hand, apartheid was a marketplace aberration, and more liberal businesspeople hoped that unregulated "market forces" would eventually rectify racial imbalances. Sections of business did lobby for changes to apartheid (whose rigidity, especially in restricting free movement and settlement of blacks, limited their potential profits) but undoubtedly, corporations in mining, manufacturing, and agriculture benefited from super-low black wages throughout the apartheid period.

The 1948 election result came as a shock to many people in South Africa who had expected the reelection of the venerable leader of the governing United Party, General Jan Smuts. Mandela was "stunned and dismayed." However, although the result heralded future pain and devastation for black communities, Oliver Tambo told Mandela that the election of the National Party on an apartheid platform would at least help to clarify in the minds of many Africans their political enemy, making mass mobilization by the ANC easier.[18]

The victory of the National Party and its hasty promotion of harsh apartheid policies pushed the ANC in a radical direction. Now the Youth League saw itself well placed to undermine Xuma's moderate position. In December 1949, Mandela and other Youth League leaders met with Xuma, urging the ANC President-General to accept the League's Program of Action, which put forward the need for boycotts, strikes, and civil disobedience if the government remained intransigent to the demands of the overwhelming majority of the people. The League, recalled Mandela in a

1991 interview, wanted Xuma to lead in civil disobedience as Mahatma Gandhi had done (both in South Africa and later in India).[19]

After Xuma once more failed to agree to militant policies, the Youth League put forward an alternative slate of candidates for the ANC national conference held a few weeks later, and their candidates were victorious. The new leadership, now including Mandela's mentor Walter Sisulu as secretary-general, adopted the radical Program of Action endorsing boycotts and strikes. It was a decisive shift in African politics. Mandela, now working for a law firm and unable to get time off, was unable to attend this momentous conference, held in Bloemfontein, capital of the Orange Free State and many hours away by train. However, the new action-oriented ANC would soon appoint him to its National Executive Committee to fill the resignation of Xuma in March 1950. The "changing of the guard" and the victory of the Youth League were complete.

The 1940s was a turbulent decade. Rapid urbanization and sharply deteriorating conditions of life of many Africans combined with the harsh application of racially discriminatory laws and disillusionment with post-war government policies to produce a situation ripe for the emergence of the Congress Youth League and the radicalization of Nelson Mandela.

As 1950 began, the National Party pushed ahead with unseemly haste to impose its apartheid policies. In February, at the youthful age of only 32, Mandela joined the ANC's highest body, the National Executive Committee. A gargantuan struggle between two diametrically opposed political forces a fiercely antiblack government determined to separate the races, and an increasingly militant African nationalism that for the first time in its history assumed a mass character—would epitomize the decade of the 1950s. This mass movement was now to be dominated by the fiery eloquence and amazing organizing abilities of Nelson Mandela, as he quickly blossomed into the most widely known and respected black leader across the length and breadth of South Africa.

NOTES

1. Nelson Mandela, *Long Walk to Freedom: The Autobiography of Nelson Mandela* (Boston: Little, Brown, 1994), pp. 85–86; "Congress Youth League Manifesto" (1944), in *Freedom in Our Lifetime: The Collected Writings of Anton Muziwakhe Lembede*, ed. Robert Edgar and Luyanda ka Msumza (Athens: Ohio University Press, 1996), p. 65.

2. Luli Callinicos, *Oliver Tambo: Beyond the Engeli Mountains* (Cape Town: D. Philip, 2004), p. 143.

3. Anthony Sampson interviewed in the film *Mandela: Son of Africa, Father of a Nation*.

4. "Congress Youth League Manifesto," p. 58.

5. Mandela, *Long Walk to Freedom*, p. 84; "Comments by Oliver Tambo, November 1973," in Carter Karis Collection, Center for Research Libraries, Chicago, 2:XM33:96/2.

6. Mandela, *Long Walk to Freedom*, pp. 84–85; "Constitution of the ANC Youth League 1944," in Thomas Karis and Gwendolen M. Carter, eds., *From Protest to Challenge: A Documentary History of African Politics in South Africa 1882–1964*, vol. 2 (Stanford: Hoover University Press, 1973), pp. 309–314.

7. Ezekiel Mphahlele, *Down Second Avenue* (London: Faber, 1959), pp. 162–163; Mandela, *Long Walk to Freedom*, pp. 88–92; Fatima Meer, *Higher than Hope: The Authorized Biography of Nelson Mandela* (New York: Harper, 1990), pp. 39–41; Anthony Sampson, *Mandela: The Authorized Biography* (New York: Knopf, 1999), p. 38.

8. *Report of the Witwatersrand Mine Natives' Wages Commission on the Remuneration and Conditions of Employment of Natives on Witwatersrand Gold Mines* (Pretoria: Government Printer, 1944); African Mine Workers Union. *Statement Submitted to the Witwatersrand Gold Mines Native Wages Commission* (1943).

9. Youth League, "The African Mine Workers Strike: A National Struggle," 1946, in A. B. *Xuma Papers*, Center for Research Libraries, reel 4; Mandela, *Long Walk to Freedom*, p. 89.

10. Ismail Meer, *A Fortunate Man* (Cape Town: Zebra Press, 2002), p. 121; Mary Benson, *South Africa; the Struggle for a Birthright* (London: IDAF, 1985), p. 95; Sampson, *Mandela: The Authorized Biography*, p. 10.

11. Mandela, *Long Walk to Freedom*, pp. 90–91.

12. Callinicos, *Oliver Tambo*, pp. 155, 159.

13. Meer, *Higher than Hope*, p. 46; Ahmed Kathrada, *Memoirs* (Cape Town: Zebra Press, 2004), pp. 67–68.

14. Tom Lodge, *Mandela: A Critical Life* (New York: Oxford University Press, 2006), p. 252 gives a joining date of 1942, but there is no hard evidence. Given his earlier attendance at ANC rallies and a common African tendency to support ANC aims, Mandela probably simply identified with the ANC from around 1942.

15. Meer, *Higher than Hope*, p. 43.

16. T. D. Moodie, *The Rise of Afrikanerdom* (Berkeley: University of California Press, 1975); Deborah Posel, *The Making of Apartheid 1948–61* (Oxford: Clarendon, 1991); Leonard Thompson, *The Political Mythology of Apartheid* (New Haven, CT: Yale University Press, 1985).

17. Patrick Furlong, *Between Crown and Swastika: The Impact of the Radical Right on the Afrikaner Nationalist Movement* (Hanover, NH: Wesleyan University Press, 1991).

18. Mandela, *Long Walk to Freedom*, p. 97.

19. Mandela interview with Steve Gish, 1991 cited in Steven Gish, *Alfred B. Xuma: African, American, South African* (New York: New York University Press, 2000), p. 160.

Chapter 5

NO EASY WALK TO FREEDOM: DEFIANCE OF APARTHEID

Some South Africans remember the 1950s as a lively decade of fast cars and glamorous movie stars and musicians. The black musical *King Kong*, with its electrifying young singer Miriam Makeba, was a great hit, and the popular magazine *Drum* built a wide readership with a heady mix of glamour and politics. However, this also was a watershed period in South African history that saw intense political contestation over the future direction of the country. For Nelson Mandela and the ANC, together with its allies, this would involve a protracted struggle aimed at the winning of civil rights for blacks and the defense of democratic rights for all South Africans in the face of increased government repression as the all-white National Party steamrolled its harsh apartheid policies.

Mandela would be right in the middle of these dramatic events, increasingly directing very large-scale protests—in some ways akin to the role played by Martin Luther King in the United States. This chapter describes and explains Mandela's rise to national leadership in the ANC and his active role as a major organizer of protests against the ever-increasing onrush of apartheid legislation. The escalating political turbulence of the time would make it very difficult for Mandela to balance his political engagements with his professional life as a lawyer and family commitments, but he would emerge by the middle of the decade as one of South Africa's most prominent leaders.

By now a tall, handsome young man of great personal charm, Mandela in many ways epitomized these fabulous, fiery fifties. His reputation as a defender of black rights soared through his legal work as an attorney and his high profile as a political leader. After becoming a member of the

ANC's peak body, the National Executive Committee, Mandela increasingly asserted his claim to leadership through his eloquence and his organizing abilities. To understand not only the motivation for his actions but also the severe constraints under which he would operate, it is necessary first to see just how pervasive and repressive apartheid was becoming.

The structure of apartheid rested on a formidable armory of racially discriminatory laws. By the early 1950s, many of the legislative pillars of this edifice were in place. Demographically, the Group Areas Act of 1950 forced blacks to live in separate, rigidly designated areas. The Population Registration Act arbitrarily classified all citizens by race. The 1953 Reservation of Separate Amenities Act tightened "petty apartheid" to avoid as far as possible contact between the races; for example in buses, on beaches, and in post offices. In the economic sphere, there was no escape for blacks: the Bantu Building Workers Act made it a criminal offense for Africans to perform undesignated skilled work; the Native Labour (Settlement of Disputes) Act of 1953 prohibited strikes by black workers; and the Industrial Conciliation Act repressed black labor unions. Politically, the government whipped up paranoia in the white community claiming a total onslaught from both a "red menace" and a "black peril." One after another, these draconian laws rolled off the statute book, with no effective white opposition and with blacks now completely excluded from voting or representation.

The noose of apartheid continued to tighten. Education of black youth suffered greatly as apartheid's architect, Verwoerd, introduced the 1953 Bantu Education Act, which created an inferior education system based upon a menial syllabus that saw Africans merely as "hewers of wood and carriers of water." Later in the decade, the Extension of University Education Act would prevent black students attending "white" universities and created separate race-defined educational institutions. Many books were banned and censorship was intense and ham-fisted, leading to absurd situations such as the banning of the children's book *Black Beauty* and the tardy introduction of television (permitted only in the 1970s), which was anathema to the conservative Afrikaner fear of "Western" corruption of their ultra-Calvinist morals. In architecture, vast triumphalist monuments such as the Voortrekker Museum symbolically trumpeted the victory of white supremacy.

The pass laws, common before the apartheid period, now became even more restrictive, with arrests of thousands of ordinary Africans on the flimsiest of infractions, often accompanied by their super-exploitation on forced labor farms. In the 1950s, journalists Henry Xhumalo and Ruth First exposed this forced labor on the potato farms of the rural town of Bethal in the pages of *Drum,* whose editor, Anthony Sampson, had befriended Mandela.

The effects of apartheid would be truly monumental. Forced removals of Africans from their homes would displace millions and create family upheavals, trauma, and substantial economic losses. The impact of apartheid on African women, many of them forced into largely infertile rural backwaters with little working opportunities or health facilities, was particularly devastating. Apartheid also operated at the personal level, adversely affecting the daily lives of all black peoples. Individuals were subjected to humiliating pass laws and pseudoscientific tests were used to classify people into four groups: White, Black, Indian, and Colored. The intrusion of apartheid into private life even extended to sex and religion. Social apartheid was enforced by the Prohibition of Mixed Marriages Act and Immorality Amendment Act, which prohibited interracial marriage or sex. Authorities could even legally bar Africans from church services if considered "a nuisance." Under these conditions, psychological traumas proliferated.

All these draconian measures motivated and energized Mandela to protest—along with tens of thousands of other South Africans appalled by the attacks on democracy and human rights. Mandela would soon lead popular anti-apartheid opposition in the large-scale Defiance Campaign and against forced removals and demolition of multiracial neighborhoods, but first he needed to harmonize his political ideas with those of the majority of his fellow activists and measure these ideas against practical possibilities for their success.[1]

In early 1950, the narrow interpretation of African nationalism then dominant in the Youth League still influenced Mandela. He vigorously opposed a one-day general strike called for May 1, 1950 by the Defend Free Speech Convention and endorsed by some leading members of the ANC and by the Communist Party. He clashed bitterly with young Indian communist Ahmed Kathrada over the strike, claiming it represented a dilution of the African nationalist struggle. However, Mandela was changing. Over the next few months, influenced by Sisulu's more inclusive African nationalism, and increasingly aware that effectively combating the powerful apartheid onslaught would require the broadest possible unity, Mandela began to broaden his stance. Before long, Kathrada would become one of his closest and dearest friends.[2]

The Suppression of Communism Act, passed soon after, was couched in very broad terms to cover any form of determined opposition. After the Communist Party itself was banned, the act would be used against all manner of other political opponents of the regime, from liberals to labor organizers, and it was later extended to church leaders. Quickly, Mandela came to appreciate the need for allies. Particularly impressed by the dedication to the ANC of African communist Moses Kotane, Mandela began to read widely about colonialism and Marxism. While never becoming a communist, Mandela saw the practicality of Marxist philosophy's dialectical materialism and the appropriateness to African conditions of its dictum, "From each according to one's ability to each according to their needs." He began to pepper his speeches with references to imperialism and capitalism, if remaining essentially an African nationalist. By this time, he reconciled with the majority view in the ANC that supported unity in action with other anti-apartheid organizations, whether African, white, or Indian, and irrespective of political shade.[3]

Accordingly, over the next two years Mandela's support within the ANC rose. He replaced Xuma on the ANC National Executive Committee and in 1951 became president of the Congress Youth League. In the following year, members elected him president of the Transvaal African Congress, the largest and most powerful provincial branch of the ANC. His eschewing of internal political squabbles and his growing stature as an eloquent and strong speaker made him attractive as a leader, confirmed in his major role in fighting unjust laws.

Mandela was the coordinator of the massive 1952 Campaign of Defiance against Unjust Laws. Before the main campaign in June, there were large demonstrations on April 6, 1952, a date symbolically marking 300 years of white oppression. As Youth League president, he addressed an overflowing crowd in "Freedom Square" in Johannesburg. Referring to hundreds of telegrams of support received from organizations from as far apart as America, India, China, and Australia, Mandela declared that freedom-loving youth of all races in South Africa would join in the battle for peace and liberty.[4]

The systematic enrollment of thousands of special volunteers, each of them committed to nonviolent civil disobedience, now began. Mandela addressed many of the volunteers, impressing on them the need for strict adherence to the discipline of nonviolence and avoidance of retaliation if provoked. Such an approach was very much in the style of Mahatma Gandhi, but with one important difference. Mandela's view that nonviolence was a *tactic* appropriate for the time and not a general, overriding principle prevailed over the pure Gandhian outlook of the Mahatma's son Manilal, who still lived in South Africa. Mandela's tasks were onerous: he was responsible for the organization, national coordination, and financing of what would turn out to be the largest-ever campaign of the ANC to date. Four days before it began, he drove hundreds of miles to the port city of Durban where, as the main speaker, he addressed ten thousand people: it was, he remembered, "an exhilarating experience" to speak before such a crowd.

On June 26 (now commemorated as Freedom Day in South Africa), the main campaign began in earnest. Thousands of protestors challenged the rigid segregation of apartheid, entering restricted townships and "whites-only" service points at post offices and railway stations. Police arrested hundreds as jails overflowed. On the opening day, Mandela traveled to the town of Boksburg near Johannesburg to launch the campaign in the northern province of the Transvaal. That evening, police arrested him while walking in the street, even though he was not demonstrating. Inside the prison van, he pondered the impact of his enforced absence on the progress of the campaign, but was heartened by his fellow prisoners' spirited singing of the African national anthem, *Nkosi Sikelel' iAfrika* ("God Bless Africa"). Released on bail, Mandela resumed his coordinating role, traveling around the country explaining tactics, and encouraging firm but disciplined action. The protests grew nationwide and lasted six months, involving some 8,500 volunteers, with many more offering their support. Another important task Mandela had to coordinate was material assistance to the dependants of arrested volunteers, a difficult proposition given the very limited financial resources of the ANC.

The Defiance Campaign failed to move apartheid's leaders to repeal unpopular laws. However, it mobilized thousands of protestors, many of whom subsequently joined the ANC, transforming it from a body of about 20,000 into—for the first time in its history—a mass-based African nationalist movement of some 100,000 people. These activists also lost their fear of jail and learned practical lessons in organizing. ANC growth was particularly rapid in the large Eastern Cape coastal cities of Port Elizabeth and East London. In these cities, isolated and random acts of violence not linked to the campaign marred an otherwise generally peaceful operation.

The government counterattacked. In July 1952, Mandela and many other leaders of the ANC and its allies found themselves arrested. In December, a magistrate found them guilty of the deliberately vague crime of "statutory communism" (meaning in effect, opposition to the government) and gave them a suspended sentence. Further attacks, and bitter defeats, were to follow, one after the other.

The apartheid government used the Group Areas Act to reclassify the vibrant black and multicultural neighborhood of Sophiatown as a whites-only zone. In June 1953, heavily armed police forcibly evicted some 58,000 residents, many of whom had lived in the suburb for many years.

Mandela's banning order had now expired, freeing him temporarily for political action. He joined the Sophiatown-based English priest Father Trevor Huddleston, of the monastic order Community of the Resurrection, in efforts to mobilize popular opposition to the forced removals. Evictions began very early in the morning. Mandela rushed to support the residents, but the force was overwhelming; police leveled machine guns. Huddleston remonstrated with the police but to no avail as Mandela helped calm the crowd. The apartheid government consummated its victory by renaming the neighborhood *Triomf* (Afrikaans for "Triumph").[5]

More defeats followed. The introduction of Bantu Education saw mission schools, which had historically dominated the formal schooling of Africans, forced to close or hand over their schools to the apartheid government. Hundreds of thousands of black students now faced the prospect of no alternative but to participate in a clearly inferior education system. As in Sophiatown, Mandela and the ANC were largely powerless to stop the full force of the state. Efforts to form community-based and ANC-organized African schools with nonracial and democratic curricula attracted some support among families. However, without resources to back up the idea, parents eventually if reluctantly had no choice but to send their children to the new segregated schools.

Fearful of Mandela's growing popularity and his unwillingness to compromise with institutionalized state racism, the apartheid government sought once more to silence him. In September 1953, Mandela again received a banning order. Then the government tried to force him to resign from the ANC, further curtailing his political work. He was, however, still able to give advice as a lawyer, and he continued to operate underground wherever possible, helping to teach secret political classes.

In this period, although very busy in the day-to-day organizational tactics of the anti-apartheid movement, Mandela also had to think strategically. As a result, he began to write political articles for the press and for the ANC. Given his incessant banning orders, writing became an effective outlet for his energy. He wrote articles for *Drum* and for the ANC-aligned magazines *Liberation* and *Fighting Talk*. Mandela's succinct, punchy, and inclusive style would become a hallmark of his speeches and writings. This is evident in one of his first pieces, a short article he wrote for *Drum* in August 1952 about the aims of the Defiance Campaign. In it, he stressed that the ANC was opposing not a particular people, whites, "but a system which has for years kept a vast section" of Africans in bondage. Mandela's inclusivity is apparent in his welcoming of "true-hearted volunteers from all walks of life without consideration of colour, race, or creed."[6]

Concern for the predicament of his people and an astute understanding of what to do about it are apparent in Mandela's writings of this time. In a 1955 article, "People Are Destroyed," he vividly sketches the tormented lives of Africans dragooned onto prison labor farms. Here we can imagine Mandela the lawyer arguing passionately for his clients. In another essay, written for *Fighting Talk,* on whose editorial board he sat, Mandela condemned the way in which the government had cajoled the traditional leaders of the Transkei Bhunga (advisory council) into accepting the "Bantustan" project. This policy divided black South Africans, often artificially along ethnic lines, and forced them into poverty-stricken "tribal homelands," an early form of the sort of policies elsewhere that in later years would become widely known as "ethnic cleansing."[7]

Mandela's predictions in these writings were ominous and prescient: "Cabinet ministers are arming themselves with inquisitorial and arbitrary powers to destroy their opponents and hostile organizations. . . . All constitutional safeguards are being thrown overboard and individual liberties are being ruthlessly suppressed." His solution was unity, and his message graphic, invoking Holocaust images: "The specter of Belsen and Buchenwald is haunting South Africa. It can only be repelled by the united strength of the people of South Africa."[8]

During this period Mandela was deeply influenced by the growing Africa-wide and worldwide movements for freedom and independence of colonial peoples. India was already independent, and it was increasingly apparent that many African countries would soon follow. Mandela's Presidential Address on September 21, 1953 to the Transvaal ANC encapsulated the spirit of the times. Over the decades, the very title of this speech, "No Easy Walk to Freedom," would become a leitmotif of Mandela's own, and South African's national, struggle for freedom. The title phrase is in fact from an article by Indian freedom fighter Jawaharlal Nehru: "There is no easy walk to freedom anywhere, and many of us will have to pass through the valley of the shadow (of death) again and again before we reach the mountain tops of our desires."[9] Delegates thunderously received the moving speech, but a government order banning him from attending meetings for six months meant that a colleague had had to read the speech on his behalf.

Freedom was the hallmark of the address. Africans, he wrote, have "been banned because we champion the freedom of the oppressed people of our country and because we have consistently fought against the policy of racial discrimination in favor of a policy which accords fundamental human rights to all, irrespective of race, colour, sex or language." Yet if Mandela stressed the growing repression by the apartheid state, he also pointed to the "new spirit and new ideas" of the opposition. Today, he stated, "The people speak the language of action" and, invoking the Defiance Campaign added, "There is a mighty awakening among the men and women of our country."[10]

The Cold War was affecting Africa, and in his address, Mandela referred to a rising tide of colonial repression and anticolonial resistance in countries such as Kenya, Tanganyika (later Tanzania), and Vietnam. Independence of several Asian nations had encouraged Africans to fight for their own freedom and the early 1950s saw bitter conflicts begin in Kenya, Algeria, and other countries. Mandela's organization, the ANC, spoke out forthrightly on these matters. Mandela singled out massacres of Kenyans by British forces. He trenchantly criticized Britain and America for siding with French and Portuguese colonial empires and for failing to support the African fight for freedom. He also strongly endorsed world peace, warning of the threat of nuclear war.

The ANC now appointed Mandela as first deputy president under their new leader, Chief Albert Luthuli. A popular Zulu traditional leader, Luthuli was a devout Christian, but the government pressured him to resign from the ANC and, when he refused, dismissed him as chief. Mandela got on well with Luthuli, but government repression made it harder for the ANC leadership to function effectively. Mandela's banning order stipulated that he could not meet with more than one person at a time, inducing severe psychological stress: "Banning not only confines one physically, it imprisons one's spirit," he later commented.[11]

In response to the banning orders, and convinced that the apartheid government inevitably would ban the ANC, Mandela devised an ingenious way to combat further repression. The "M-Plan" (or "Mandela-Plan") proposed a closely-knit, locally based, street-by-street form of resistance to an increasingly repressive state. The M-Plan centered on a basic unit composed of a street with 10 houses led by a steward, a structure that would allow seamless transmission of decisions from the ANC leadership to members and the speedy replacement of banned leaders from within its ranks. The ANC adopted Mandela's model. Its leadership began to meet in secret and launched for its members political education courses at which Mandela lectured. However, although the M-Plan would prove useful when the African liberation movement went underground after 1960, in the 1950s, it lacked a detailed structure or paid organizers and therefore was not able to resist the full force of government repression later in the decade.

Simultaneously with all this intense political activity, Mandela's legal career began to blossom. After serving his legal articles, he passed the final qualifying examination to become an attorney and started to work for the law firm of H. M. Basner, a long-time supporter of African civil rights. A few months later, in 1952, Mandela opened his own law office and soon invited his old friend Oliver Tambo, who was also now a lawyer, to join him in the practice. Set in the heart of downtown Johannesburg and strategically located directly opposite the Magistrate's Court, their office soon became very popular among African clients.

A handful of African lawyers such as Alfred Mangena and Pixley Seme had plied their trade in previous decades, but this new firm, "Mandela and Tambo," was effectively the only African law practice in town, and it immediately resonated with the swelling tide of black resentment against the escalating arrests under the plethora of new apartheid laws. Africans particularly reviled the harsh and racist enforcement of the pass laws. Facing arrest at any time of day and night, mere lack of correct documentation could see them jailed or removed from the city. "It was a crime to walk through a Whites Only door, a crime to ride a Whites Only bus, a crime to use a Whites Only drinking fountain, a crime to walk on a Whites Only beach," lamented Mandela.[12]

Because of this ongoing repression, Mandela and Tambo were never short of clients, who each morning crowded its small offices and overflowed into surrounding corridors. At times, they handled up to seven cases in a single day. Some clients traveled hundreds of miles from rural areas to visit the renowned young black lawyers, who quickly developed a professional reputation for honesty, commitment, and courage to take on the white-dominated South African legal system.

The duo had complementary legal qualities and contrasting appearances: the diminutive Tambo, always cool under pressure, polite, even gentle, but unrelenting and forceful in his pursuit of justice; Mandela, tall and regal, emotive but eloquent and equally committed to fairness. The politically committed attorneys, while charging fees for serious cases such as murder and robbery, often gave their legal services gratis to fellow activists. Mandela's quick thinking and audacity in the courtroom is evident in one of his memorable case victories. Defending an African domestic worker charged with theft of clothes of a white "madam," Mandela confronted the madam with an alleged pair of stolen panties, asking if they were hers. She was too embarrassed to admit ownership and the court dismissed the case. In a similar case, a magistrate dismissed an alleged rape when, under cross-examination from Mandela, a white woman refused to admit she had suffered sexual penetration; again, something too embarrassing to admit within the confines of white society of the time.[13]

Mandela's two lives, professional attorney and rising political star, complemented each other. Everywhere he saw confirmation of his political belief in the need for real socioeconomic and political change: widespread poverty and extreme racial discrimination that was destroying the lives of his people. To rub salt into his wounds, Mandela knew that in the rigid racial hierarchy of apartheid, and despite only being in his 30s, he had already reached the summit of the legal profession for an African. He could work as an attorney but never aspire to be a prosecutor, magistrate, or judge.

Mandela had studied and worked with many progressive white lawyers, some of whom, such as the legendary advocate George Bizos, also worked with his firm. But the weight of an unsympathetic officialdom hung over his work. In 1954, Mandela's suspicions of racism within the legal profession heightened when the Transvaal Law Society asked the South African Supreme Court to strike him from its roll because of his political challenges to apartheid laws. Mandela won the case but increasingly, as he faced more and more banning orders, his legal partner Tambo had to pick up much of the legal work in their region, as Mandela was restricted from traveling beyond the Johannesburg magisterial district.

By 1955, the apartheid regime was pushing ahead with its gigantic forced social engineering programs that would earn it international opprobrium as a polecat among nations. Despite the government's political victories, the ANC with its leaders like Mandela stood resolutely in its way, refusing to submit to the complete loss of their rights and dignity. Faced by an impassive government based on minority rule, the ANC and its allies decided to stage a massive show of democratic feeling, the Congress of the People.

Mandela was deeply involved in organizing the Congress of the People, which adopted the hugely influential Freedom Charter, but once more police banned him from attending an important event. The idea for a gathering representative of all the people of South Africa, to present their demands for the kind of South Africa they wanted, had come from Z. K. Matthews, a moderate leader of the ANC in the Cape Province and previously one of Mandela's lecturers at Fort Hare. Preparations for the Congress had been widespread across the country, with thousands of ordinary people sending in their political demands and their hopes for the future, sometimes scrawled on bits of paper or cigarette packs. Delegates would incorporate these demands into the wording of the Freedom Charter, adopted when the Congress of the People finally met at Kliptown, a poverty-stricken neighborhood near Johannesburg, on June 26, 1955.

The Freedom Charter called for a future South Africa that would be inclusive, belonging to all who lived in the country, and it embraced a nonracialist democracy. In clear contradistinction to the divisiveness of apartheid, the simple yet moving language of the Charter asserted national unity. The Charter's goals resonated, much like key American political documents such as the Constitution and Bill of Rights, with the majority of South Africans whose demands it largely reflected. Given the Charter's importance, it is worth reproducing its central tenets. The preamble declared:

> We, the People of South Africa, declare for all our country and the world to know:
>
> - that South Africa belongs to all who live in it, black and white, and that no government can justly claim authority unless it is based on the will of all the people;
> - that our people have been robbed of their birthright to land, liberty and peace by a form of government founded on injustice and inequality;
> - that our country will never be prosperous or free until all our people live in brotherhood, enjoying equal rights and opportunities;
> - that only a democratic state, based on the will of all the people, can secure to all their birthright without distinction of colour, race, sex or belief;
> - And therefore, we, the people of South Africa, black and white together as equals, countrymen and brothers adopt this Freedom Charter;
> - And we pledge ourselves to strive together, sparing neither strength nor courage, until the democratic changes here set out have been won.

The Charter then set out the goals of the people:

- The People Shall Govern!
- All National Groups Shall Have Equal Rights!
- The People Shall Share in the Country's Wealth!
- The Land Shall Be Shared Among Those Who Work It!
- All Shall Be Equal Before the Law!
- All Shall Enjoy Equal Human Rights!
- There Shall Be Work and Security!
- The Doors of Learning and Culture Shall Be Opened!

- There Shall Be Houses, Security and Comfort!
- There Shall Be Peace and Friendship!

Under these goals, many idealistic and practical objectives were enumerated.

- All laws which discriminate on grounds of race, colour or belief shall be repealed;
- All people shall have equal right to use their own languages, and to develop their own folk culture and customs;
- Restrictions of land ownership on a racial basis shall be ended, and all the land re-divided amongst those who work it to banish famine and land hunger;
- Men and women of all races shall receive equal pay for equal work;
- People shall not be robbed of their cattle, and forced labor and farm prisons shall be abolished;
- The colour bar in cultural life, in sport and in education shall be abolished; Education shall be free, compulsory, universal and equal for all children. . . .

The Freedom Charter concluded with a rousing call: "Let all people who love their people and their country now say, as we say here: THESE FREEDOMS WE WILL FIGHT FOR, SIDE BY SIDE, THROUGHOUT OUR LIVES, UNTIL WE HAVE WON OUR LIBERTY."

One section of the Freedom Charter—"The People Shall Share in the Country's Wealth"—took on a left-wing tinge, particularly through its calls to nationalize industries. This policy was due in part to the crucial role in its drafting by the radical Rusty Bernstein and in part to the emergence of a more formal Congress Alliance. However, the radical calls for social justice were also in part due to the continuing impoverishment of the black majority; the overwhelming majority of Africans remained either wage earners or rural toilers. This socialistic aspect of the Freedom Charter would be both a blessing and curse for Mandela and the ANC as on the one hand, it helped build working-class support, yet on the other hand, it alienated many conservatives at home and abroad. In general, however, the Charter became a rallying point for most opponents of apartheid.

The following year, Mandela wrote a rather visionary article describing the significance of the Freedom Charter in *Liberation*, the magazine of the Congress Alliance. This new alliance united not just the ANC and its old ally the South African Indian Congress, but also the newly formed Congress of Democrats, a white progressive organization, and from 1955 the South African Congress of Trade Unions. If such a united front developed, Mandela argued, the Freedom Charter would "be transformed into a living instrument and we shall vanquish all opposition and win the South Africa of our dreams during our lifetime." In years to come, the Freedom Charter's significance would indeed grow enormously, becoming a sort of "Bill of Rights" of the anti-apartheid forces for a future free South Africa. Mandela would later refer to it as being "born of our struggle and rooted in South African realities"; it "received international acclaim as an outstanding human rights document." Over the long years of imprisonment that lay ahead, the Charter would be a guide to action and a beacon of hope for Mandela.[14]

Mandela's personal life also was changing in many ways. In early 1952, he learned to drive for the first time and purchased his first automobile, at the time a "luxury" available only to the tiny African elite. This new acquisition made him, in his own words, "a one-man taxi service" for friends and political comrades. He returned to his favorite sports, boxing and jogging, working out in an improvised gym in the township of Orlando. As his sons grew up, he would delight in taking them with him to the gym. Mandela's social networks were widening, and he befriended the popular jazz group *The Manhattan Brothers*. At this time, American cultural influences, especially music and Hollywood movies, were increasing in South Africa. Black South Africans often saw successful role models in African Americans, and this was reflected in the names of musical groups.

Through such cultural and sporting contacts and activities, Mandela sought to become an "ordinary" person. In reality, however, he was far from ordinary. Joe Matthews, a fellow ANC activist of the 1950s, described Mandela as always wanting to seem just "one of the crowd," yet always standing out with his noble and imposing bearing. The Mandela family doctor, Nthatho Motlana, who characterizes Mandela as "kingly," backs up this viewpoint.[15]

The Mandela family saw two new arrivals. Their second son, Makgatho Lewanika, was born in 1950, followed in 1954 by a daughter, Pumla Makaziwe. The intense demands of politics on his time forced Mandela to somewhat overlook his family. His preoccupation with ANC affairs was so great that his eldest son, Thembi, even asked Mandela's wife Evelyn where his father lived! Mandela later "rued the pain I had often caused my family through my absence." He recalled, "I did not in the beginning choose to place my people above my family, but in attempting to serve my people, I found I was prevented from fulfilling my obligations as a son, a brother, a father and a husband." In many ways, this was an unconscious development born of his increasing political commitments to the African people as a whole. Events also forced it upon him. That the banning order served on Mandela in 1953 prevented him even from attending his son's birthday party reflected the absurdity of apartheid. Using one of his favored boxing metaphors to explain his predicament, Mandela mused that he had moved from being an "untested lightweight" in the ANC to its "light heavyweight division" where he now "carried more pounds and more responsibility."[16]

Similarly, Mandela had to neglect his extended family affairs back in the rural Transkei. However in 1955, after his ban of two years had been lifted, he planned a brief working holiday back there—his last holiday had been eight years earlier—in which he hoped to combine a family reunion with political discussions with Transkeian traditional leaders Chief Sabata and Chief Daliwonga. He recalls that his daughter Pumla Makaziwe, then only two years old, had awoken at midnight as Mandela was preparing for the trip and asked if she could accompany her father, inducing pangs of guilt from Mandela. On the trip, Mandela was able to visit his mother and sister, but his attempts to dissuade his relative Kaiser Matanzima to oppose the government-imposed Bantustan system failed.

Mandela's rural past evoked memories that he tried to impart to his children. With his sons now in elementary school in Orlando, Mandela would drive them to school. Mary Benson, who knew him personally in this period, recounts how one day driving them to school Mandela slowed down to show them some horses, perhaps reflecting his yearning for another, rural world beyond "Orlando's bleak landscape of regimented little block houses, under a permanent pall of smoke from the innumerable cooking fires."[17]

Although far away from his birthplace, Mandela kept in touch with his relatives and clan through their visits. Luvuyo Mtirara was the son of the chief who had replaced Mandela's father. Though 10 years younger than Mandela he had had grown up with him in Thembuland. When he and other clansmen visited "Mandela the lawyer" in Johannesburg, they felt great pride that a clan member was now the most respected black lawyer in the land. Mandela's prestige as a black lawyer was so high that clients of all ethnic backgrounds visited his office; many would even wait at his home. His dedication was unmistakable: Oliver Tambo's wife Adelaide characterized Mandela as "a very forthright person, a very strong leader, a man with a very sympathetic ear towards other people's difficulties. . . . He always had time for everybody."[18]

By the middle of the decade, South African politics had reached an impasse. On the one hand, the government was too powerful and too obstinate to dissuade or dislodge. It skillfully manipulated Afrikaner nationalism in the white electorate to stay in power, and systematically got rid of its opponents. On the other hand, popular opposition to apartheid was growing rapidly. Over the next few years, anti-apartheid protests would widen still further to include large numbers of women and organized labor. In all this tumult, Nelson Mandela's popularity among Africans and among the broad democratic forces of all races would continue to rise. He would presently see big changes not just in his political but also in his personal and family life.

However, the dust had scarcely settled from the presence of the thousands who had gathered for the Congress of the People before Mandela, together with 155 of his colleagues, would be fighting for their very lives, charged with high treason.

NOTES

1. *Mandela: An Audio History*, 1: "The Birth of Apartheid (1944–1960)": http://www.radiodiaries.org/mandela/mstories.html.

2. Ahmed Kathrada, *Memoirs* (Cape Town: Zebra Press, 2004), pp. 67–68.

3. Nelson Mandela, *Long Walk to Freedom: The Autobiography of Nelson Mandela* (Boston: Little, Brown, 1994), pp. 104–105.

4. "The Struggle Has Begun," *Spark* (Johannesburg), April 11, 1952.

5. Mary Benson, *Nelson Mandela* (London: Penguin, 1986), p. 58; Trevor Huddleston, *Naught for Your Comfort* (New York: Doubleday, 1956).

6. Nelson Mandela, "'We Defy'. Ten Thousand Volunteers Protest against 'Unjust Laws,'" *Drum*, August 1952.

7. Mandela, "People Are Destroyed," *Liberation*, October 1955; "Bluffing the Bunga into Apartheid," *Fighting Talk*, 1955. Many such articles appear in edited collected writings such as *No Easy Walk to Freedom* (New York: Penguin, 2002) and *The Struggle Is My Life* (London: IDAF, 1990), and on the ANC Web site: http://www.anc.org.za/people/mandela/index.html.

8. Mandela, "People Are Destroyed."

9. This phrase comes from Jawaharlal Nehru, "A Survey of Congress Politics, 1936–39," in Nehru, *The Unity of India: Collected Writings 1937–1940* (London: Drummond, 1941), p. 131.

10. *No Easy Walk to Freedom* (New York: Penguin, 2002) reproduces the speech; it is online at http://www.anc.org.za/ancdocs/history/mandela/1950s/sp530921.html#1.

11. Mandela, *Long Walk to Freedom*, p. 126.

12. Mandela, *Long Walk to Freedom*, p. 130; Luli Callinicos, *Oliver Tambo: Beyond the Engeli Mountains* (Cape Town: D. Philip, 2004), pp. 172–179.

13. Mandela, *Long Walk to Freedom*, p. 133; Benson, *Nelson Mandela*, p. 57.

14. Nelson Mandela, "Freedom in our Lifetime," *Liberation*, June 1956, online: http://www.anc.org.za/ancdocs/history/campaigns/cop/freedom-in-our-lifetime.

html; Jennifer Crwys-Williams, ed., *In the Words of Nelson Mandela* (New York: Penguin, 1997), p. 28.

15. Joe Matthews and Nthatho Motlana, interviewed in the film *Mandela: Son of Africa, Father of a Nation*.

16. Mandela, *Long Walk to Freedom*, pp. 105, 125; *In the Words of Nelson Mandela*, p. 24.

17. Benson, *Nelson Mandela*, p, 54.

18. Mandela, *Long Walk to Freedom*, pp. 153–154; transcription of interview of Peter Davis with Luvuyo Mtirara, Transkei, 1985, Peter Davis Collection, Black Film Center-Archive, Indiana University; Adelaide Tambo interviewed in *Remember Mandela!* (Vancouver: Villion Films, 1988).

Mandela as a young man. Courtesy of UWC-Robben Island Museum Mayibuye Archives.

Mandela the boxer, 1950s. Courtesy of UWC-Robben Island Museum Mayibuye Archives.

Wedding of Nelson and Winnie Mandela, 1958. Courtesy of UWC-Robben Island Museum Mayibuye Archives.

Mandela in African (Thembu) dress, while underground between 1961 and 1962. Courtesy of UWC-Robben Island Museum Mayibuye Archives.

Mandela and Sisulu on Robben Island, 1960s. Courtesy of UWC-Robben Island Museum Mayibuye Archives.

Nelson Mandela and his wife Winnie, walking hand in hand, raise clenched fists upon his release from Victor prison, Cape Town, Sunday, February 11, 1990. The African National Congress leader had served over 27 years in detention. (AP Photo).

In retirement: Nelson Mandela with Desmond Tutu, July 2005, Johannesburg. Photo courtesy of Nelson Mandela Foundation.

Two presidents: Nelson Mandela with his successor, Thabo Mbeki, 2006, at the Nelson Mandela Annual Lecture. Photo courtesy of Nelson Mandela Foundation.

Chapter 6

ON TRIAL, WINNIE, AND THE "BLACK PIMPERNEL" GOES UNDERGROUND

High treason! All around South Africa in the early hours of December 5, 1956, security police arrested the leaders of the anti-apartheid alliance. Mandela was one of the first arrested, bundled into a police car as his small children watched in helpless confusion.

In a short time, 156 leaders of all races from political, women's, and labor organizations faced arraignment on charges of high treason. Incarcerated in the foreboding Fort Prison in Johannesburg for 16 days, police humiliated them by forcing them to strip naked for hours in a prison yard. The clearly political trial would drag on for five years, effectively removing from public life the regime's main opponents, notably Nelson Mandela. Yet Mandela somehow found ways around these very serious legal impediments not only to survive but also to launch an important new phase of the anti-apartheid struggle—and even to start a new family.

Apartheid repression had intensified. Numerous repressive laws tightened the vise of control as the government accelerated its new version of earlier colonial policies of "divide and rule" over Africans. The Bantu Authorities Act of 1951 and later the Promotion of Bantu Self-Government Act of 1959 arbitrarily classified black people into ethnic groups each with a separate "homeland," a move that eventually would deny blacks even their South African citizenship. These forcibly imposed spatial arrangements were unusually severe and even bizarre. Over the next three decades, the authorities would round up and forcibly remove tens if not hundreds of thousands of urban Africans to "Bantustans," some of which, such as Bophuthatswana or KwaZulu, comprised dozens of separate pieces of territory with no common frontier. Largely poverty-stricken women, children, the sick, and the elderly inhabited these isolated, often infertile regions, ruled by government-appointed "tribal" leaders. Things were little better in the cities, where widespread poverty and overcrowding, extremely low wages, high mining mortality rates, repressed labor unions, endemic crime, and ongoing mass arrests under the pass laws made the lives of the majority of Africans harsh and dangerous. Mandela immediately came out strongly against the measures.

Popular opposition to the regime continued to rise as antidemocratic and racist laws rolled off the statute books in quick succession. New forces now joined Mandela's ANC. In August 1956, a large and peaceful demonstration of some 20,000 women of all races, led by the Federation of South African Women (formed in 1954) and the ANC Women's League, marched to the administrative seat of government, the Union Buildings in Pretoria. Their spokespersons, Lilian Ngoyi and Helen Joseph, presented a petition with over 100,000 signatures protesting against restrictive passes forcibly imposed on African women. The refusal of Prime Minister Johannes Strijdom even to meet with the women sparked off further demonstrations across the country; it also gave rise to a popular song:

Strydom, wathint'abafazi	Strydom, You have touched the women
Wathint'imbokodo	You have struck a rock
Uzakufa.	You have dislodged a boulder, you will die.

Such determined resistance delayed for seven years the introduction of passes for African women.[1]

Although there had been earlier, and effective, women's protests against the carrying of passes, often seen as a virtual badge of slavery, the rise of a mass-based women's political movement was a new development in South African politics. Early ANC constitutions had treated women as mere nonvoting "auxiliaries." In the 1950s, however, the ANC Women's League helped mobilize women, who joined in much larger numbers. The legal, social, and economic marginalization of African women continued to limit their entrance into politics, but ANC men such as Mandela now had to deal politically—and personally—with women on a more egalitarian basis.

The other major nonracial organization to emerge at this time, the South African Congress of Trade Unions, also worked closely with the ANC, but the government quickly silenced many labor leaders. Nevertheless, these nonracialist bodies directly challenged the racially segregated society that the apartheid leaders sought to construct on a colossal scale not seen since the European totalitarian regimes of the 1930s. These organizations, together with members of the Congress Alliance, were living proof that an alternative to apartheid was possible. The leaders of all these movements would join Mandela as defendants in the Treason Trial, held in the historic building that once housed the Old Synagogue in Pretoria.

Ironically, the common incarceration of leaders of all races and diverse political persuasions during the Treason Trial cemented unity among people previously divided by segregation and isolated by restrictive banning orders. The charges were simple, if based on flimsy evidence: the accused had planned the Congress of the People and drawn up the Freedom Charter, which an increasingly paranoiac government—operating at the time of the Cold War—deemed a communistic, treasonous document inciting the people violently to overthrow the government. There was of course nothing of this sort in the Freedom Charter, but the government used legal procedure to draw out proceedings for five years and stifle the democratic movement.

Mandela did his best to exploit the trial to highlight the lack of democracy and the human rights abuses by the apartheid regime. Initially, the state's case was so weak that the court dismissed charges against all but 30 of the defendants for lack of evidence. Mandela was among those still arraigned. Oswald Pirow, accused in earlier years of being a Nazi sympathizer, led the prosecution. The defense team fielded a distinguished attorney, Vernon Berrangé, who argued that far from being treasonous, the Freedom Charter enshrined ideas "shared by the overwhelming majority of mankind of all races." Eventually, in March 1961, the Supreme Court of South Africa overturned all the remaining charges because the state did not establish any "revolutionary" intent in the actions of the accused. Indeed, in his trial defense in August 1960, Mandela had made clear that, if given proof of the government's serious willingness to move towards implementing universal voting rights, even on a staggered basis, then he was quite amenable to compromise and calling off mass protests. Throughout the Treason Trial, Mandela demonstrated his deep understanding of and commitment to the rule of law and parliamentary democracy and to the traditions of legal procedure and peaceful protest. He also made clear that the ANC was "not anti-white, we are against white supremacy," and that the ANC even had support from some white South Africans.[2]

On one level, exoneration was a success for Mandela and his coaccused. But on another level, it would herald an even more draconian government policy that would thumb its nose at any kind of legal constraint on its political agenda. During the first few years of the Treason Trial, there had been an element of civility, even chivalry, between the black political prisoners and their white captors, something quite common in South Africa given the many years of living side by side under colonial rule. Mandela and his police minders could still joke and make small gestures of humanity towards each other, and the judiciary still maintained some semblance of independence. After 1960–1961, however, police and courtroom attitudes were to harden as apartheid leaders moved more and more toward implementing a rigid authoritarian state that would brook no dissent.

For Mandela, the Treason Trial had important effects, both positive and negative. On the one hand, in prison and in legal defenses, he grew closer to his people and to other leaders. He increasingly appreciated the commitment of progressive white and Indian South Africans to a free, nonracial, and democratic alternative to apartheid. He came to know white activists such as the English-born Helen Joseph, a leader of the Federation of South African Women. On the other hand, the effects of the trial contributed significantly to the break-up of his marriage and family and devastated his legal practice.

Family affairs suddenly crowded back into Nelson Mandela's life. Since 1952, relations with his wife Evelyn had steadily grown weaker, and then acrimonious as she recoiled from his intense politicization. Her conversion to become a Jehovah's Witness did not help matters as far as Mandela was concerned, and she appears to have demanded that he choose between her and the ANC. The Treason Trial probably was the final straw; Mandela was so deeply involved in fighting for his life that he probably either was not fully aware of the irreversible nature of the split or else had decided it was now inevitable. When released on bail at Christmas 1956, Mandela found she had moved out of the house for good, taking the children—and, he noticed, even the curtains—with her, only visiting Mandela once during the trial. Divorce followed in March 1958.[3]

With the legal firm of Mandela and Tambo in terminal decline due to their enforced absence at the Treason Trial, and with his family life in tatters, Mandela was under enormous psychological and financial strain, but he received inspiration from an unexpected quarter. He fell in love—from his own account at first sight—with a vivacious, forceful, and beautiful young social worker who would become his partner and political companion for three decades.

Nomzamo Winifred ("Winnie") Zanyiwe Madikizela, herself later to become a significant political activist, was born on September 26, 1934 at Bizana, in rural Pondoland. Like Mandela's, her family was of some noble lineage but of modest means. In addition, like Mandela, her given name would be prophetic: "Nomzamo" means "she who will undergo trials."

Winnie Madikizela had a strict upbringing, against which she rebelled. Her mother, whom she once described as a "religious fanatic," was a domestic science teacher who died when Winnie was young. Her father, like her mother, was a stern disciplinarian as well as a teacher, and with entrepreneurial skills. Despite his lack of physical affection toward her, upon the death of her mother she helped him run the household. She credits him with teaching her about the history of African oppression.[4]

Moving to Johannesburg in January 1953, Madikizela completed a diploma at the Hofmeyr School of Social Work in Johannesburg, of which Nelson Mandela was a patron. She then became the first African medical social worker at Baragwanath Hospital in Soweto. Her politicization began gradually. She had heard of Mandela and his 1952 Defiance Campaign while a student; and when undertaking research in Alexandra, where Mandela had lived in the 1940s, she saw with her own eyes the very high rate of black infant mortality. The ANC Women's League mobilization against passes increasingly politicized Winnie Madikizela, and with the Treason Trial on everyone's lips, she naturally heard more and more about Nelson Mandela. In the American-owned hostel in which she stayed, in the evenings she would hear factory workers singing freedom songs about him.

Winnie Madikizela's beauty and charm, education, and probably her growing political consciousness, transfixed Nelson Mandela after they chanced to meet in March 1957. Characteristically, he asked her to help him raise funds for the Treason Trial families, and in keeping with custom, sent a friend to fetch her for a meal. He ordered his favorite spicy curries for them both, initially a dish much too hot for her simple rural tastes, but with the help of his Indian South African friends (from whom he had cultivated the taste), it was one she soon mastered.

Mandela's conservative relative, Kaiser Matanzima, increasingly moving toward an accommodation with the apartheid regime over Bantustans, had himself recently been courting Winnie with letters. However, soon she was seeing Mandela regularly. During a picnic, and after explaining the many dangers involved in his work, he proposed. At first, she stood in awe at this rising political colossus. At the wedding feast, held in her home in Bizana on June 14, 1958, her father warned that she was marrying "the struggle." They had two weddings: in the Methodist Church in Bizana, and then a traditional Xhosa ceremony in the countryside. The couple made the most of their brief happy days together—the police had granted Mandela only four days leave. Back in Johannesburg, the Treason Trial soon enveloped him, but he somehow found time for family life. He would pick up Winnie from her work in his Oldsmobile car and they set about establishing a home. Before too long, they had two daughters, Zenani, born on February 5, 1959, and Zindziswa ("Zindzi") on December 23, 1960.[5]

Unlike Evelyn, Winnie identified openly with Nelson Mandela's political struggle. She regularly attended sessions of the Treason Trial and became active in the Orlando West branch of the ANC and the ANC Women's League; so much so, that she soon began to develop her own independent political persona, greatly inspired by Women's League legends such as Lillian Ngoyi. In 1958, Winnie Mandela's participation in the League's anti-pass campaign led to her first arrest, a month of detention with 600 other women, sleeping on a crowded concrete floor. The physical brutality of jail nearly caused Winnie to lose her first child, with whom she was pregnant; fortunately, she received support from Walter Sisulu's wife, Albertina, a trained nurse. Like her husband, Winnie suffered banning orders—the first in 1962 restricting her to Soweto.

All these experiences—arrests, her awareness of poverty and despair, threats to her husband and family, and police harassment (which was to continue unabated over many decades, and which she steadfastly resisted)—engendered in her a deep hatred of apartheid. She recounted to an American writer three decades later in 1985, that at first

> I was bewildered like every woman who has had to leave her little children clinging to her skirt. . . . I cannot, to this day, describe that constricting pain in my throat as I turned my back on my little ghetto home, leaving the sounds of those screaming children as I was taken off to prison. As the years went on, that pain was transformed into a kind of bitterness that I cannot put into words.[6]

Despite shared politics and the obvious romance and deep mutual attraction of the couple's relationship, their time together was restricted greatly. Winnie was lucky to see him once a week during the trial. In an autobiographical note written while on trial for his life in 1964, Mandela related that after his discharge from the Treason Trial in March 1961 the ANC leadership instructed him to go underground in early April and that he had "never been home since." The stolen weekends together, Winnie would say in 1989, would not even add up to six months: "I've never had the opportunity to live with Mandela. . . . I have never really known what married life is. I have always known him as a prisoner."[7]

With one marriage in ruins, and a second marriage greatly circumscribed by banning orders and political imperatives, Mandela felt pangs of remorse for his family. Richard Stengel, the American writer who collaborated with Mandela on his autobiography, remarked in a 1999 Public Broadcasting Service (PBS) interview that unlike most other famous figures, Mandela admitted to many regrets: "That's what makes him a big man." In particular, Mandela regretted how political events had forcibly diminished his role in his own family, "as a father, as a husband, and as a son." He also was emotional about his mother, who in this period just could not understand why the state was criminalizing her son. As well, Mandela regretted the dissolution of his first marriage, and the resulting estrangement from his children by that marriage.[8]

In spite of all the personal and legal obstacles, Mandela adapted effectively to his enforced banishment from formal politics. He learned to master communicating indirectly with his people and published numerous press articles affirming the rights of Africans to the vote and for land rights and decent working conditions. In this period, Mandela wrote many influential articles for the anti-apartheid press. In the magazine *Liberation*, he wrote sharp pieces attacking the foundations of apartheid, such as Bantu Education and the Bantustan scheme. However, freedom of the press for opponents of apartheid was declining rapidly. The main newspaper supporting the Congress Alliance, *The Guardian* (1937–1963) faced repeated government banning orders and despite cleverly adopting successive name changes, finally went under in 1963.

Mandela also mastered the art of meeting covertly. Despite his never-ending banning orders, he was able surreptitiously to get together with other ANC leaders. In 1958, after meeting secretly with the leadership, he agreed to the abandonment of a three-day stay-away protest after harsh police repression on the first day. In October of the same year, he surreptitiously communicated to the ANC Women's League his advice that their members jailed for anti-pass demonstrations should apply for bail, not leave themselves open to further harm by remaining too long in prison.[9]

Problems of a different kind also now confronted Mandela. Tensions had been growing between the majority of ANC supporters, who supported the Freedom Charter with its emphasis on fighting for a united South Africa of all races, and those in the movement still favoring an Africanist political strategy of Africans "going it alone" (which Mandela himself had finally discarded a few years earlier). The cultivation by the ANC of wider alliances with white and Indian forces in 1959 finally precipitated a split, spawning the Pan Africanist Congress (PAC). The new body sought to differentiate itself from the ANC in both domestic and foreign policy. The ANC had adopted a broad anticolonialist and anti-imperialist platform, and in 1958, Mandela had drawn attention to what he and many other African nationalists perceived as the replacement of European imperialism by a more subtle American neocolonial influence.[10]

In contrast, PAC policy was rather confused, holding its founding meeting in the United States Information Office in Johannesburg, but then courting Communist China. The PAC would never achieve the same level of mass support as the ANC, but the division would plague the South African liberation movement for decades and complicate its task of building international solidarity. Mandela, like many other ANC leaders, was fiercely opposed to the breakaway, although there would be times when his diplomacy and conciliatory personality would serve to smooth over political divisions.

The ANC's new rival, the PAC, did gain some support and in 1960 they sought to preempt an ANC anti-pass campaign. In Sharpeville, south of Johannesburg, they called a major demonstration. Police opened fire on unarmed protesters, killing at least 69, many shot in the back attempting to flee.[11]

The momentous events of the Sharpeville Massacre opened a Pandora's box of political conflict. A week later, Mandela demonstratively burned his passbook, the badge of black subjugation, in public before journalists in Orlando. Other Congress Alliance leaders did the same. Two days afterward, police arrested Mandela and other leaders under a newly announced state of emergency. In April 1960, the apartheid regime intensified repression, banning the ANC and PAC and provocatively calling a general mobilization of the armed forces. Deep in the countryside in Pondoland, where Winnie Mandela and Oliver Tambo had grown up, the government deployed armored cars against rural peoples demonstrating in their thousands for representation in parliament; more and more people called on the ANC to arm them for protection. The government had drawn a line in the sand.

Mandela watched these events helplessly from prison. After his release from prison at the end of August 1960 he toured the country, ostensibly to close down branches of the ANC Youth and Women's Leagues given the organization's banning, but also to discuss the possibilities for an underground opposition movement to apartheid. After a short respite, when his daughter Zindzi was born just before Christmas, he was off again on another grueling round of talks, including to the nearby country of Basutoland (now Lesotho).

There was one more chance of forcing a relatively peaceful transition to democracy: mass action. With the ANC banned, Mandela's focus became a new ad hoc body, the All-in African Conference. It met in

Pietermaritzburg, Natal Province, with the aim of drafting a new demo-cratic constitution in defiance of the government. Given that his nine years of consecutive banning orders were due to expire, he was convinced that he soon would face their renewal. He therefore went into hiding, reemerging to make a dramatic, surprise appearance at the conference, after which the ANC National Executive Committee directed him to go underground.

Facing virtual martial law, and with their political movements banned and strike action by Africans effectively illegal, the All-in African National Action Council, with Mandela as secretary, called a three-day "stay-at-home" protest. The idea was to protect African workers from retribution by their simply not going to work, rather than striking. From underground, Mandela issued numerous calls for workers to observe the action. Using cunning disguises and great audacity, and moving quickly from one "safe house" to another, he thwarted persistent police attempts to arrest him. The press thus dubbed Mandela the "Black Pimpernel" (a take on the elusive adventurer, the Scarlet Pimpernel, during the time of the French Revolution).

Writer Mary Benson witnessed the unfolding events: "At night heli-copters flew low over the townships, flashing searchlights down on to houses to frighten the occupants. Police announced they would force peo-ple to go to work and employers threatened to sack those who responded to Mandela's call." Benson joined journalists in a meeting with Mandela at a secret location in a modest white neighborhood. He was, she recalled, "far from conspiratorial, relaxed in striped sports shirt" with "eyes closed to slits as laughter reverberated through his huge frame." However, as they left, Mandela grew grave and ominously declared that if the government responded only with naked force then the ANC's traditional nonviolent policy would have to be reconsidered.[12]

As Mandela had anticipated, the government replied to the peace-ful stay-at-home protest with a massive show of force. He wrote at the time from a hideaway in Soweto that despite the huge size of the protests, which dwarfed simultaneous state efforts to celebrate the declaration of South Africa as a republic, the government saw fit to rush through a law allowing detention without bail or charge. Further, the government had mobilized the army and had armed groups of white civilians, deployed police in African townships, banned meetings, and arrested some 10,000 Africans. Mandela had no choice but to call off the protests on the second day. He declared, "Terror and intimidation became widespread. Only by adopting these strong-arm measures could the government hope to break the stay-at-home." He ended his report on a defiant tone, announcing the

launching of a countrywide campaign of noncooperation with government aimed at achieving a democratic constitution. Significantly, he also
echoed the call made a year earlier by ANC President Albert Luthuli for
international sanctions. "We ask our millions of friends outside South
Africa to intensify the boycott and isolation of the government of this
country, diplomatically, economically, and in every other way." Later in
the year, he made a sober, if prophetic prediction: South Africa was now
in a state of perpetual crisis, which would grow more acute.[13]

The ANC, and Mandela, had reached a Rubicon. Over the next few
weeks, Mandela and Sisulu agreed, and convinced the ANC leadership,
that there was now no viable alternative to fighting fire with fire: armed
struggle was necessary. Even ANC President Luthuli, the 1961 recipient
of the Nobel Peace Prize and a firm proponent of majority rule by constitutional means, whom secretly Mandela had consulted, agreed reluctantly
that the government had closed off all peaceful avenues to change. Luthuli's
comments when the government had dismissed him from the chieftaincy
in 1952 for refusing to resign from the ANC now seemed never more appropriate: "Who will deny that 30 years of my life have been spent knocking
in vain, patiently, moderately and modestly at a closed and barred door?"[14]

In what would be the last available media recording of his voice for
29 years, a British television journalist in May 1961 captured Mandela's
foreboding and prescient views.

> There are many people who feel that the reaction of the govern-
> ment to our Stay-at-Home, ordering a General Mobilization,
> arming the white community, arresting tens of thousands of
> Africans . . . notwithstanding our clear declaration that this
> campaign is being run on peaceful, and non-violent lines,
> closed a chapter as far as our methods of political struggle are
> concerned. . . . [We] feel that it is useless and futile for us to
> continue talking peace and non-violence against a govern-
> ment whose reply is only savage attacks on an unarmed and
> defenseless people.[15]

Already in the 1950s, Mandela and Sisulu had discussed the theoreti-
cal probability of this move given the intransigence of the regime. Now
they faced the prospect, with virtually no military training or experience,
of organizing an armed challenge to a powerful, seemingly impregnable
government.[16]

A new organization emerged, the armed wing of the national liberation movement known as *Umkhonto we Sizwe* (Spear of the Nation, or

simply MK). Mandela had suggested the name, and it was he who led the MK High Command, which also included Walter Sisulu, Joe Slovo, and Govan Mbeki. Mandela was following in the footsteps of those historic African resistance leaders about whom he had heard as a child and youth over the campfire and at school.

For most of 1961, Mandela lived "on the run" in "safe houses" such as the inner-Johannesburg apartment of Wolfie Kodesh, a Jewish communist. In October, disguised as a gardener, he moved to the Lilliesleaf farm in Rivonia, outside Johannesburg, where MK based its High Command. Organizational matters occupied much of his time: discussion of strategy and tactics, experiments with explosives, and traveling around the country to establish branches of MK and plant the seeds of underground resistance. However, occasionally, as at Lilliesleaf farm, Mandela was able to meet briefly, if at great peril, with Winnie and the children. Many years later in prison on Robben Island, he would remember how his young son Thembi had visited him at a safe house, "wearing an old jacket of mine that came to his knees. He must have taken some comfort and pride in wearing his father's clothing, just as I once did with my own father's. When I had to say good-bye again, he stood up tall, as if he were already grown, and said, 'I will look after the family while you are gone.'" There were, however, to be very few more of these family encounters.[17]

From the beginning, Mandela and other MK leaders agreed that they should avoid human targets at all cost. Given the strategic weakness of MK—it lacked weapons, South Africa was surrounded by sympathetic, fellow white supremacist or colonial regimes that would offer no sanctuary to guerrillas, and much of the country was unsuitable for guerrilla warfare in any case—MK leaders decided sabotage offered the best way to highlight the predicament of Africans while avoiding loss of life. MK's main thrust was to combine military with political struggle to overthrow Nationalist Party rule and white supremacy, and win "liberty, democracy and full national rights for all the people of this country." On December 16, 1961, rather appropriately on the anniversary of a bloody historical defeat of Africans celebrated by white South Africans, the sabotage campaign began.[18]

In the meantime, the ANC had decided shortly after facing banning to send some of its top leaders, notably Oliver Tambo, across the border to freedom and exile. Yet, leadership inside the country also was crucial, and Mandela therefore decided to remain inside South Africa. At the same time, building international support was another priority, and successful military resistance would require both training and material aid. The successful example of newly independent African countries, some of whom had fought long, bitter wars of national liberation against colonial powers, inspired Mandela.

Without seeking permission of the government, who would have refused in any case, Mandela in January 1962 crossed the border into the British colony of Bechuanaland (in 1966 to become independent as Botswana) and then traveled on to gain support across Africa. After visiting Tanganyika (later Tanzania), Sudan, and Nigeria, he addressed the Pan-African Freedom Movement of East, Central and West Africa conference in Addis Ababa, Ethiopia. Extensive tours of North Africa with ANC veteran Robbie Resha, and of West Africa with Tambo, and then a three-week trip to England followed. Not just the progress of newly independent African countries but also the rapid establishment of ANC overseas diplomatic bases impressed Mandela. He worked hard to build support among African leaders, some of whom would become his strongest allies. In Africa, he received strong political and sometimes financial support, but the focus of his work soon turned squarely to military affairs.[19]

In Algeria in March 1962 and in Ethiopia from June to July, Mandela undertook limited basic and strategic military training that would be necessary to launch and direct an armed challenge to the apartheid state. Soon, however, Sisulu called him back to South Africa, where he consulted with ANC leaders about his trip.

Two weeks later, in August 1962, the extraordinary exploits of the Black Pimpernel, during which time he had evaded police for 17 months, finally ended. Security police arrested him on a road north of Pietermaritzburg as he drove disguised as a chauffeur of Cecil Williams, a white supporter. Incarcerated in Johannesburg's Old Fort until his trial in October, Mandela faced charges of incitement of strikes and illegally leaving the country.[20]

In the face of such a grave challenge, Mandela responded with a mixture of eloquence and courtroom drama. Dressed African-style in a fine jackal-skin kaross draped over his shoulder, he raised a clenched first and shouted "Amandla!" (Power). A judiciary "controlled entirely by whites," he argued, was not impartial, and he did not feel morally or legally bound to obey laws made by a parliament in which Africans had no representation whatsoever. "The white man makes all the laws, he drags us before his courts and accuses us, and he sits in judgment over us." Mandela's rhetoric was to no avail. The government banned the widespread protests against his arrest and in November 1962, he received a sentence of three years imprisonment.[21]

Sent to Pretoria Central Prison, Mandela immediately asserted his human rights and dignity, refusing the short pants officials mandated Africans to wear—a further symbol of their alleged "childishness" and "inferiority." As a result, prison authorities forced him into solitary confinement. However, later Mandela was able to mix with the other prisoners. In May 1963, he was moved for the first time to Robben Island, a foreboding and isolated prison-isle, somewhat resembling Alcatraz.

Without Mandela, the MK High Command continued to plan armed and political resistance to apartheid but, like Mandela, it was not as cautious as it might have been. In July 1963, security forces detected the MK base at Rivonia and arrested the leadership. Mandela was already in prison, but the wealth of incriminating documents found at Rivonia also implicated him. Even more than in the Treason Trial, Mandela and his compatriots now were truly fighting for their lives.

The Rivonia Trial lasted from 1963 to 1964. The court charged Mandela and his co-accused with conspiring to overthrow the apartheid regime by violent revolution. Death was the likely result. Defense attorney Joel Joffe, who later exposed the racism faced in court by the accused, was not optimistic, but Mandela's own eloquent speech from the dock—lasting one and a half hours, delivered in a calm but resolute voice, and unflinching—may well have made the difference between life and death.[22]

In his courtroom address, faced by accusations of plotting revolution, Mandela freely conceded that, given his people's dire poverty, Marxism's goal of a classless society had impressed him. South Africa, he noted, was the richest country in Africa, but whereas whites enjoyed a very high standard of living, Africans "live in poverty and misery." Moreover, the avenues out of this poverty—education and skills—were legally barred to Africans, destroying their human dignity, while hundreds and thousands of pass law arrests each year destroyed family life. Yet Mandela was careful to balance his radical rhetoric with his characteristic legalism. He demonstrated his great respect and admiration for American and British institutions, the Bill of Rights and U.S. Congress, and the Magna Carta and the British Parliament. Mandela made a moving plea for the rights of Africans: they wanted a living wage; to choose their own work; to live and travel where they wished and to own their own land; to live with, and not be separated from, their families. "Above all," he added, "we want equal political rights, because without them our disabilities will be permanent. I know this sounds revolutionary to the whites in this country, because the majority of voters will be Africans. This makes the white man fear democracy." Mandela's response to the charges was characteristically defiant; "The Government should be in the dock, not me, I plead not guilty." The closing words of his the speech from the dock immortalized his opposition to apartheid:

During my lifetime I have dedicated myself to this struggle of
the African people. I have fought against white domination,
and I have fought against black domination. I have cherished
the ideal of a democratic and free society in which all persons
live together in harmony and with equal opportunities. It is an
ideal which I hope to live for and to achieve. But if needs be, it
is an ideal for which I am prepared to die.[23]

The penultimate phrase, "if needs be," inserted on the advice of fellow-
accused Govan Mbeki into the speech that Mandela himself had written,
appears to have moved the judge, who sentenced the Africans accused
not to death but to life imprisonment, inducing an enormous and audible
feeling of relief in the packed, electrically charged courtroom.[24]

Winnie, leading Mandela's aged mother by the hand, came to the trial
along with many of his family, friends, and comrades. Mandela had urged
his kin to attend dressed in traditional attire to make a statement that
this trial was really about African freedom. Winnie and Mandela himself
appeared dramatically in stunning African clothes. It was, remarked an
old friend from the Transkei, a moving affair. "I told him, 'Go to prison,
but we expect you back.' I told him I would slaughter a cow in his honor
when he returned, whenever that would be." It would be a very, very long
time.[25]

In the period 1956 to 1964, Mandela emerged as the most popular and
famous opponent of apartheid. A wide range of Africans, from the middle class to urban workers and rural peasants, all began to see in him hope
for a better life. His close friend Oliver Tambo in December 1964 wrote
from the ANC's new headquarters in exile, in Dar es Salaam, Tanzania,
of Mandela's qualities:

As a man Nelson is passionate, emotional, sensitive, quickly
stung to bitterness and retaliation by insult and patronage. He
has a natural air of authority. He cannot help magnetizing a
crowd: he is commanding with a tall, handsome bearing; trusts
and is trusted by the youth, for their impatience reflects his
own; appealing to the women. He is dedicated and fearless. He
is the born mass leader.[26]

Mandela had faced increasingly difficult times as apartheid repression
intensified. The long drawn out Treason Trial from 1956 to 1961 may
have resulted in the exoneration of all the accused, but it wore down the
resources of the ANC. Soon after came the Sharpeville Massacre and

then the banking of the ANC, forcing Mandela underground, where he headed the fledgling military resistance. His underground exploits as the "Black Pimpernel" further enhanced the aura around his leadership, but finally his arrest and sentencing to life imprisonment in the Rivonia Trial appeared to mark a watershed in South African politics. Ahead lay the sternest challenge of his life: long, bleak years on a cold, windswept prison island where the apartheid authorities hoped his compatriots and the world would forget him. However, Mandela's famous speech from the dock when sentenced clearly indicated that he was not only prepared for the worst, but also fully prepared to continue the resistance to apartheid in yet another different arena.

NOTES

1. Francis Meli, *South Africa Belongs to Us: A History of the ANC* (Bloomington: Indiana University Press, 1989), pp. 132–133; Helen Joseph, *Tomorrow's Sun: A Smuggled Journal from South Africa* (New York: John Day, 1967), chapter 3.

2. Nelson Mandela, "Courtroom Testimony," in *Mandela, Tambo and the ANC: The Struggle against Apartheid*, ed. Sheridan Johns and R. Hunt Davis Jr. (New York: Oxford University Press, 1991), pp. 68–69; Tom Lodge, *Mandela: A Critical Life* (New York: Oxford University Press, 2006), p. 70; Mandela, *The Struggle Is My Life* (London: IDAF, 1990), p. 93.

3. Transcripts on Mandela, "Husband and Lover," in *The Long Walk of Nelson Mandela*: http://www.pbs.org/wgbh/pages/frontline/shows/mandela/husband/; Martin Meredith, *Nelson Mandela: A Biography* (New York: St. Martin's Press, 1998), p. 147.

4. Winnie Mandela, *Part of My Soul* (New York: Viking Penguin, 1985); Diana Russell, *Lives of Courage: Women for a New South Africa* (New York: Basic Books, 1989), chapter 6; Emma Gilbey, *The Lady: The Life and Times of Winnie Mandela* (London: Cape, 1993).

5. Nancy Harrison, *Winnie Mandela: Mother of a Nation* (London: Gollancz, 1985); discussion with Ursula Vassen, a fellow social worker and friend of Winnie, East Lansing, MI, June 2007.

6. Russell, *Lives of Courage*, pp. 101–103. See also interview with Adelaide Tambo by Peter Davis, January 19, 1985, Peter Davis Collection.

7. Mandela, *The Struggle is My Life*, pp. 270–271; Russell, *Lives of Courage*, p. 105.

8. See the online transcript of a 1999 interview with Richard Stengel: http://www.pbs.org/wgbh/pages/frontline/shows/mandela/husband/stengel.html.

9. For the texts, see http://www.anc.org.za/ancdocs/history/mandela/1950s/.

10. Mandela, "A New Menace in Africa," *Liberation*, March 30, 1958, pp. 22–26, and online at: http://www.anc.org.za/ancdocs/history/mandela/1950s/.

11. Philip Frankel, *An Ordinary Atrocity: Sharpeville and Its Massacre* (New Haven, CT: Yale University Press, 2001).

12. Mary Benson, *A Far Cry* (New York: Viking Penguin, 1989), pp. 128–129.

13. Mandela, *General Strike: A Report of the 3-Day Strike in South Africa (May 29, 30, 31, 1961)*, July 1961: http://www.anc.org.za/ancdocs/history/mandela/pr610603.html; Mandela, "Out of the Strike," in *Africa South in Exile* 6, no. 1 (October 1961), pp. 15–23.

14. Mandela, *Long Walk to Freedom*, p. 125, citing Luthuli, *Let My People Go* (New York: McGraw Hill, 1962), p. 235.

15. Copy of speech, Peter Davis Collection. The clip features in many films on Mandela.

16. Bernard Magubane, Philip Bonner, Jabulani Sithole, Peter Delius, Janet Cherry, Pat Gibbs, and Thozama April, "The Turn to Armed Struggle," in *The Road to Democracy in South Africa* (Cape Town: Zebra, 2004), pp. 53–145.

17. Mandela, *Long Walk to Freedom*, p. 390; Meredith, *Mandela*, p. 197.

18. Howard Barrell, *MK: The ANC's Armed Struggle* (London: Penguin, 1990), p. 3.

19. Mandela to Maggie Resha on the death of her husband, in M. Resha, *'Mangoana Tsoara Thipa ka Bohaleng: My Life in the Struggle* (Johannesburg: Cosaw, 1991), p. 241; Mandela, *Long Walk to Freedom*, pp. 256–259.

20. On the rumors of possible, although unsubstantiated, CIA informers to Mandela's arrest see Mandela, *Long Walk to Freedom*, p. 278, and Gilbey, *The Lady*, p. 61.

21. "Mandela Challenges Court's Impartiality," *The Times* (London) October 23, 1962; Mandela's trial speech, October 15, 1962, in *The State versus Nelson Mandela*, pp. 16–18, copy in Center for Research Libraries, Chicago.

22. Joel Joffe, *The Rivonia Story* (Cape Town: Mayibuye Books, 1995); Interview with Joel Joffe by Peter Davis, London, January 21, 1985, Peter Davis Collection; Hilda Bernstein, *The World That Was Ours: The Story of the Rivonia Trial* (London: SA Writers, 1989).

23. Nelson Mandela, "I Am Prepared to Die," Pretoria Supreme Court, April 20, 1964, online at: http://www.anc.org.za/ancdocs/history/mandela/1960s/rivonia.html.

24. Govan Mbeki interview by John Carlin, in *The Long Walk of Nelson Mandela*: http://www.pbs.org/wgbh/pages/frontline/shows/mandela/interviews/mbeki.html.

25. Interview with Luvuyo Mtirara, Transkei, 1985, Peter Davis Collection.

26. Oliver Tambo, Preface to Mandela, *No Easy Walk to Freedom* (New York: Penguin, 2002), p. xxiv.

Chapter 7

THE LONG PRISON YEARS: FRIENDS, FAMILY, AND GLOBAL SOLIDARITY

After midnight on June 12, 1964, Mandela and his fellow African co-accused from the Rivonia Trial found themselves shackled and then flown on an old Dakota military transport plane to Robben Island. Alcatraz—Devil's Island—Robben Island—the name was synonymous with repression and punishment. Historically, colonial authorities had banished troublesome indigenous political prisoners to prison isles. In South Africa first the Dutch, then the British colonialists had used Robben Island, 8.7 miles (14 kilometers) off the coast of Cape Town, to incarcerate African resistance fighters. Some had tried to escape but very few survived the chilly, shark-infested waters.

The prison discipline on Robben ("Seal" in Dutch) Island was harsh, even cruel. When the prisoners arrived, warder "batons rained down on us," wrote Mandela's friend Ahmed Kathrada. Most warders were Afrikaners who abused the prisoners with racist epithets such as "kaffir": one bellowed "Dis die Eialnd. Hier julle gaan vrek" (This is the Island. Here you will die). Humiliations heaped upon humiliations: warders buried some prisoners up to their faces in sand and urinated on them, or forced them to strip and jump around. Absurd forms of racial discrimination permeated everything: Africans could have only tiny amounts of meat a week; officials somehow presumed they had no "biological" need for it given their "traditional" culture. They only received short pants, while Indian or Colored South Africans received long pants. They had to sleep on the hard floor, on thin mats. Robben Island, in the South Atlantic, can be very cold in winter and the prisoners lacked basic warmth.[1]

Mandela's cramped cell was no more than six feet square. He shared the political section of the jail with his co-accused from the Rivonia Trial: Govan Mbeki, Walter Sisulu, Ahmed Kathrada, Raymond Mhlaba, Elias Motsoaledi, and Andrew Mlangeni. Daily, the prisoners had to do forced labor with picks and shovels in a lime quarry, where in summer the blazing sun reflecting on the limestone permanently damaged Mandela's eyes; yet it took three years for him to gain permission to wear sunglasses. The hard labor lasted 13 years, but it also toughened the prisoners' resolve never to submit. The outdoor work invigorated Mandela. "It felt good to use all of one's muscles, with the sun at one's back." On the daily march to the quarry, we "could see the dense brush and tall trees that covered our home, and smell the eucalyptus blossoms, spot the occasional springbok or kudu grazing in the distance."[2]

Mandela refused to take jail lying down. His resistance took many forms: uniting, inspiring, and acting as a spokesperson for the other prisoners; opposing racism and cruelty and demanding fair treatment; and communicating with the outside world, family, and friends.

He fought for basic reforms of harsh prison conditions, no matter how small and no matter how long it took him, showing his relentless pursuit of justice, his stubbornness, and his commitment. On the very first day, confronted by an aggressive warder, Mandela stood his ground and refused to be intimidated, warning the official of legal action if he assaulted the prisoners. Mandela demanded long pants; eventually he won but refused to accept them unless all other prisoners received them. Again, his persistence succeeded. In the quarry, the prisoners faced unrealistic work quotas, but Mandela comforted and advised his comrades. "Look, don't be terrorized by these demands," he told them, "work at your own pace." Again, his persistence succeeded.[3]

The prisoners were far from passive, their resistance multifaceted. There were hunger strikes, although this tactic was of limited effectiveness given the island's isolation from the mass media, something that Mandela understood; but even so, he felt he had to go along with his comrades. There were complaints against poor conditions and brutal warders. One warder, sporting a swastika tattoo, sought to make life a misery for the prisoners with incessant intimidation and charges. In response, Mandela relayed to the visiting Helen Suzman, one of the very few South African parliamentarians to take any interest in their welfare, the prisoners' demands: better and equal food and clothing; study facilities; the right to newspapers; and an end to this warder's harsh reign. For once, there was action; Suzman complained to the government, and Mandela soon saw the warden transferred.[4]

Robben Island mirrored the racism of apartheid, but the prisoners cunningly transformed the bleak jail into an unwitting "university of the struggle." At first the Rivonia prisoners, and then later on more and more ANC and MK prisoners, including an influx of militant youth after the 1976 Soweto Revolt, all took educational courses to develop their technical skills and focus their minds. Encouraged by Mandela, many took the opportunity to gain degrees or high school diplomas through external courses. However, many books and certain subjects, such as political science, remained prohibited.

The prisoners also constructed their own elaborate forms of political education, in which Mandela was prominent as a teacher, writing messages in the white sand of the island and leading discussions. This resistance strengthened their unity and allowed a small measure of control over their lives; after a while, prison authorities abandoned efforts to prevent them from talking and let the discussions continue.[5]

Among the other underground leaders who joined the Rivonia prisoners was Mac Maharaj, who arrived six months after Mandela. Maharaj probably suffered the most physical torture of all the prisoners; before trial, he had refused to talk to his tormentors, and on "The Island," he remained defiant. He vividly recalls how "Madiba" remained a leader of the nation despite being in prison. Mandela exercised a curious form of authority over his fellow prisoners: Maharaj never knew Mandela to give an order, but invariably Maharaj would carry out the wishes of Madiba, who always would lead by example.[6]

"The Island" (as it became known among the prisoners) could be a violent place. There were terrible beatings by warders of some prisoners, such as the poet and organizer of sporting boycotts of apartheid, Dennis Brutus, dumped in a cell one night covered with bruises and with a gunshot wound from police, inflicted not long before and still infected. The warders also sought to turn the violence of the ordinary convicts incarcerated on the island against the Rivonia prisoners, of whom they were contemptuous. In this situation, Mandela's courage, leadership, and diplomatic skills came into play as he initiated efforts to bridge the gap between the different categories of prisoners and between prisoners and jailers. Initial friction with the common law prisoners gradually gave way to shared interests. Warders slowly and grudgingly began to acknowledge the humanity of all the prisoners. They showed Mandela special respect, perhaps due to his growing international reputation, or his royal ancestry, or simply because of his huge physical stature and proud bearing.

Mandela worked hard to try to develop a united front with PAC and other political prisoners. This was not easy given political rivalries. The

PAC, whose members had arrived on the Island first, seemed to resent the growing presence of ANC prisoners. However, Mandela angled persistently to find common ground and at times was able to strengthen unity between the different organizations. In 1967, he was able to get PAC leaders to cosign a petition for better treatment of all prisoners.

The mutual support of the prisoners for each other was essential to their survival. On the Island, they stealthily reproduced their outside political structures as best they could. Mandela headed the ANC's internal leadership on the Island, the High Command, or High Organ, consisting of those who had been members of the legal ANC National Executive Committee. "Kathy" (Kathrada), the youngest, built channels of communication with the different sections of prisoners. Walter Sisulu was the "beloved father" whom the others found "compassionate and always helpful." Binding them all together, and regarded by the others as their spokesperson, was Mandela.[7]

Mandela's character shines through in his relations with the other prisoners. For example, Eddie Daniels was a member of a quite different political organization, the Liberal Party, from a Colored working-class background, and had never met Mandela before coming to the Island. Looking back on their years together in confinement, Daniels stresses Mandela's integrity, foresight, compassion, tolerance, and leadership. He could be humorous, kind, and humble. Once, when Daniels was ill, Mandela personally cleaned the sick man's toilet bucket. He shared his personal letters with Daniels. Mandela would delight in calling his comrades by nicknames; it was, recalled Maharaj, a subtle way of exercising his authority. Maharaj was "Neef" (nephew), and he called Mandela "Oom" (uncle). Yet Mandela let Daniels (and very few others) call him by his private circumcision name, Dalibhunga.[8]

If, with his Thembu royal bearing, Mandela sometimes could be a little aloof, then he always took time in a fatherly way to welcome individual prisoners and discuss their problems. On Robben Island, Daniels was the lone member of the Liberal Party, already a spent force in South African politics, but Mandela insisted on treating him as an important equal. Daniels was amazed that a person of such stature as Mandela would deign to make friends with him. In prison, after coming back from important meetings, Mandela would report to the ANC and then, to protect Daniels's political integrity—as PAC members had accused Daniels of "being ANC"—he would report to him separately. Mandela was, he emphasizes, "a magnanimous man; where others ignored me—and I didn't know anyone—he was just that type of person who would come forward and embrace you and make you feel good, and extend the hand of friendship."

In part, this approach aimed to build nonracialism, to create a culture of survival on the island, and to knit the prisoners together like a family. Although political differences arose, and Mandela could be very stubborn in sticking to his beliefs, he would always say "let us work together; let us not fight one another." In this regard, states Daniels, Mandela was "a great unifier; he was never boastful, never threw his weight around."[9]

Michael Dingake was an ANC activist also jailed on Robben Island. He saw Mandela as the "most tireless participant" in the prisoners' discussions and for whom every day saw a busy routine of meetings with fellow inmates. Much of this routine involved asking about other people's welfare and complaints to such an extent that it seemed to Dingake (and other fellow Islanders, such as Kathrada) that Mandela seemed to care more for his compatriots than his own health. By insisting on their right to make complaints and by representing their interests before the prisoner authorities, Mandela empowered prisoners to present their own demands. Dingake observed Mandela's slow, purposeful style of speaking, his manner of "stressing every word, and every syllable he uttered." Mandela was a "shrewd tactician" whose close attention to detail and extensive legal experience helped blunt some of the worst excesses of cruelty carried out by prisoner officers. He would always go straight to the top with complaints about abusive treatment of the prisoners, demanding justice; in many ways, he simply wore down the bureaucracy such that it gradually conceded their rights. Mandela, a forceful and well-informed debater, also taught Dingake to see the two sides of a question.[10]

Some differences related to tactics. Mandela was pragmatic. He once shocked Daniels by musing that one day they might well have to make use of the hated Population Registration Act of the apartheid regime. Yet here, Mandela's concern was simply to ensure representation of everyone. When some prisoners said that someday they would "take care" of a notoriously cruel warder, Mandela said, "No, we may have to use him." On another occasion, Mandela encouraged fellow political prisoner Andimba Toivo ja Toivo (leader of the ANC's sister movement in the neighboring country of Namibia, SWAPO [South West African People's Organization]), not to simply walk away from wardens and opponents but to engage with them. Behind this direct or diplomatic approach to warders was pragmatism and common decency; hostility, Mandela reasoned, was self-defeating. He also had enormous self-control, which fellow prisoner and confidante Maharaj argues lay in Mandela's deep introspection and self-criticism that enabled him to think clearly and weigh all sides to an argument. Mandela also decided to learn Afrikaans, arguing it was important to know one's enemy. Why not try to educate everyone, even your enemies, he reasoned? Again, Mandela succeeded: in time, some of the warders came to respect him, and treat him with deference.[11]

One of the sharpest, if still comradely ideological tussles on Robben Island was that between Mandela and Govan Mbeki, father of Thabo Mbeki (who became South African president in 1999). One of their arguments was over the question of cooperation with apartheid-backed institutions such as the Bantustans, which Mbeki steadfastly opposed. Another was the relationship between the ANC and Communist Party. They also disagreed over whether national liberation would lead to capitalism or to socialism. Here there are clues to the policies Mandela would adopt in later decades.[12]

Survival in such a harsh prison required not just strength, endurance, and enormous willpower, but also creativity. To communicate, the political prisoners invented ingenious ruses. They collected empty matchboxes discarded by the warders, constructed false bottoms, and secreted inside them tiny written, coded messages, often written on toilet paper in milk that was normally invisible but legible if treated with the disinfectant used to clean their cells. They also forged ties with the general prisoners who delivered food, and developed a secret communication system by leaving notes under dirty dishes in the kitchen, or hidden under the rim of toilet bowls in ablutions shared by prisoners from different sections. Visitors and released prisoners also transmitted messages on their behalf: Maharaj hollowed out his study books and files to smuggle out the entire manuscript of Mandela's autobiography, secretly written in the 1970s. Another Mandela writing that Maharaj successfully hid from prison authorities was an essay written in 1976 on the future of the country. In the essay, Mandela emphasized that the major issue confronting the liberation movement was unity, something he spent much time practicing on Robben Island.[13]

The isolated prisoners particularly treasured news and education. "Newspapers," writes Mandela, "were more valuable to political prisoners than gold or diamonds, more hungered for than food or tobacco; they were the most precious contraband on Robben Island." They fought constantly for the right to have newspapers and, when refused, arranged for copies to be smuggled. They scavenged newspapers discarded by the warders. For six months, they had access to a daily newspaper after befriending, and then outwitting, an elderly night warder. On another occasion, a prisoner mischievously lifted a newspaper from the briefcase of a visiting clergyman as he prayed with eyes closed. Once, warders caught Mandela with a newspaper and he spent three days in isolation without meals. But with persistence, the prisoners secured slight improvements: from 1969, film showings; in 1975, their first hot showers; from 1980 access to news-papers; and from 1982 visits from children.[14]

The prisoners tried singing political songs in Xhosa to lighten their work, but some warders understood Xhosa, and banned singing—as well as whistling. Another important distraction became gardening. Their courtyard garden was no more than a modest patch of green in the grim, gray prison, but it gave the prisoners much needed relief from stress; it also provided tomatoes, chilies, onions, and melons. Mandela, wrote Kath-rada to family friend Tom Vassen in 1975, had become "fanatical" about the garden; it was "Nelson's baby." The arrival in the garden of a chame-leon captured the prisoners' attention and induced much debate over the peculiar nature of the creature. At other times, they turned repeatedly to discuss such curious topics as whether the tiger was native to Africa, all serving to focus their minds and avoid depression or despair.[15]

The prisoners experimented with other forms of relaxation to get their minds off their captivity. They greatly appreciated a smuggled copy of the works of Shakespeare, each of them choosing memorable lines of the Bard as their personal motto. Mandela selected a passage from the drama *Julius Caesar* that included

Cowards die many times before their deaths;
The valiant never taste of death but once. . . .

In 1975, the prisoners even staged their own play, Sophocles' *Antigone*, in which Mandela played the regal character of Creon, a role that his friend Kathrada wryly comments made up for his dethronement as island domino champion of 1973.[16]

Sport and games provided valuable recreation to reduce tension and pass the time. At first, prison authorities refused to "play ball" and denied them the freedom to play sport. However, Mandela persistently urged the International Red Cross to lobby for sports facilities, eventually granted in the mid-1970s, when volleyball equipment and a ping-pong table appeared. The prisoners developed a sophisticated sports series, including soccer and rugby tournaments. Later they built their own tennis court in the prison courtyard. Mandela did not mind that his backhand was weaker than his forearm shots; he enjoyed the relaxation. He played ten-nis and chess with Andimba Toivo ja Toivo, who many years later jested that Mandela always won and took hours to make a single chess move.

Even more than games, physical fitness was vital for well-being in a forced labor prison. In the early morning, Mandela would jog around his cell and do dozens of push-ups and sit-ups. In 1982, when he shared accommodation with other prisoners, he would rise at 3 A.M. and run around the cell for an hour, and then do aerobics and weightlifting, until finally his cellmates objected to being awakened in the middle of the night.

Despite his spirited resistance, the years on Robben Island hurt Mandela in various ways. His health deteriorated, and the psychological pressure was intense. He was distraught at the terrible news of the death of his mother and his son, Thembi. Denied permission to attend his own son's funeral, Mandela kept his grief to himself, letting only his old friend, Walter Sisulu, console him.[17]

The human isolation could be crushing. For the first years, authorities allowed Mandela only one visitor and one letter (of up to only 500 words) every six months, and prison authorities made visits very difficult for Winnie. They censored and withheld letters, but these remained a major source of hope.

Mandela cherished letters, even those arriving in tatters or blacked out by the censors: "A letter was like the summer rain that could make even the desert bloom." Visits were brief—only 30 minutes long—and with no physical contact; Mandela and Winnie had to shout at each other through thickened, opaque glass: "We had to conduct our relationship at a distance under the eyes of people we despised." It would not be until 1984 that they would have their first contact visit. To circumvent the restrictions on discussing politics, the couple invented a clever code using names only they understood: to ask about the ANC in exile, he would ask, "How is the church?" But due to police harassment and Winnie's own banning orders, he had to wait two years for her next visit. Nevertheless, Winnie worked hard, dressing elegantly and overcoming obstacles, to make every visit special for him. In a letter of November 22, 1979, he wrote to her that on a recent visit she had looked "really wonderful . . . very much like the woman I married. . . . I felt like singing, even if just to say Hallelujah!" Yet Mandela could also see the strain on Winnie. Regulations forced her to visit only via air travel, which drained her savings. When police harassment saw her lose her job as a social worker, making the financial survival of the family perilous, Mandela despaired: "My powerlessness gnawed at me."[18]

Family photographs were equally precious. He wrote intimately to Winnie in 1976 that he dusted her photograph each day, even touching "your nose with mine to recapture the electric current that used to flush through my blood whenever I did so." Three years later, in a similar letter, he told her he would have fallen apart years ago without her love and letters, and that dusting the family photos in his prison cell eased the longing. In a letter to daughter Zeni in 1977 he told her, "It's family photos, letters and family visits that keep on reminding me of the happy days when we were together, that makes life sweet and that fills the heart with hope and expectation."[19]

However, security police often refused to deliver Mandela's letters, even to his children. His letters to them exhibit a gnawing worry for their welfare, the deep pain of a father helplessly unable to be with his family. In 1970, knowing letters he had sent in 1969 had not arrived and that Winnie too was in jail, he wrote to the children that letters were a "means of passing on to you my warmest love," they helped "calm down the shooting pains that hit me when I think of you." Authorities forbade children under 18 from visiting, and they denied him permission to see his grandchildren. Years later, Mandela and Kathrada both would rue that what they missed most of all on the island was children.[20]

In the early years of his jail sentence, the mass media both inside South Africa and overseas largely forgot Mandela. The role of his wife therefore became vital to his survival and future prospects. South African journalist Benjamin Pogrund points out that "Winnie never gave up, and went on fighting to keep her husband's name alive . . . with a personal passion, standing up to the Security Police to show her contempt for them and the system they enforced." Her courage was never in doubt; she confronted armed police and berated them, but it came with a terrible cost.[21]

Arrested in 1962 and again in May 1969 without charge, Winnie Mandela was in solitary confinement for 18 months, denied bail and visitors, and brutally interrogated. On release, a massive overkill of heavily armed police rearrested and then banished her to the remote rural town of Brandfort for five years. Harassment by security forces was constant. She could not even go to church without a permit, and the only visitors allowed were a doctor and lawyer; a priest had to stay outside to give her communion. Friends such as Helen Joseph, who brought her food, faced arrest. Security police went to such absurd lengths as confiscating her bedspread, as it was in ANC colors—green, yellow, and black; 26 members of the U.S. Congress got together to send her a Pennsylvanian quilt as a replacement. Terrorists attacked the family home. In 1975, Winnie briefly resumed open political activity after her bans expired, but in a while she again was banned and sent into internal exile. Nelson Mandela tried to defend her from afar, using every legal means he could as a prisoner, employing lawyers to try to protect the family. Winnie too resisted. She broke out of isolation by interacting with local people in the poverty-stricken ghetto, helping them organize a crèche and a medical first aid program. Like her distant husband, she also developed a garden.[22]

The government interpreted Winnie Mandela's banning to extend to everyone in the house, so even her tiny daughter Zindzi could not have friends to visit. To avoid harassment, she sent her daughters to a Catholic boarding school in the nearby country of Swaziland, but the victimization continued as security police made a point of arresting Winnie whenever the children were due to return home at vacation. Her banning orders also meant Winnie could not enter her daughters' schools or speak with their teachers. Her isolation was complete, and the harsh treatment she endured from a police interrogator for seven days and seven nights, she recalls, "taught me how to hate." Explaining to her children the meaning of apartheid was painful: when six-year old Zindzi asked why her father was in jail, but not the black police officer next door, she had to clarify that in a sick society it is right for a just person to go to prison.[23]

These traumatic experiences, so typical of apartheid society, made Winnie Mandela very defensive and suspicious. She fought racial hatred with defiance and began to develop her own political following. However, her efforts to build a protective cordon around her family in the form of the "Mandela Football Club," a group of local township youth who acted as bodyguards, backfired tragically when at the end of 1989 the gang, regarding anyone who refused to join as sell-outs, was involved in the death of a youth on her premises. Mandela was distraught and the events would have momentous impact.[24]

For Nelson Mandela visits were vital to his well-being, yet the government played politics with whom they allowed to visit. Well-wishers or political supporters often could not enter the jail, while unsympathetic conservative outsiders, such as British and Australian journalists in 1964 and 1973, and an American lawyer in 1965, were able to visit and write innocuous press reports on the prison.

Family and friends remained devoted. Family physician and children's guardian Nthatho Motlana was another lifeline to the outside world. During a short, one-hour visit permitted in 1976, he found Mandela largely unchanged and unbowed, with "absolute dignity, a grand Xhosa chief! Extremely fit, mentally and physically" although his exercise was restricted: "even boxing was not allowed and he was a boxer himself!" In time, however, conditions improved somewhat, particularly when the government began to see in Mandela a possible way out of the deepening crisis in which they found themselves. By 1985, his wife was seeing him once a month.[25]

Outside Mandela's dreary prison walls, momentous changes were in the air. Apartheid had acted as a brake on socioeconomic development, greatly reducing black consumption and acquisition of skills, just as the South African economy saw deep structural changes, and the glaring contradiction between rigid racial and settlement policies and economic demands was accentuating the deep crisis; the currency plummeted.

The peoples of South Africa faced a range of other frustrations. The 1970 Bantu Homelands Citizens Act effectively denied South African citizenship to Africans forced to become "citizens" of imposed "home-lands" that were technically made "independent" states but were recognized by no countries in the world and completely under the thumb of Pretoria. Culture, heritage, and education also suffered under the impact of apartheid policies and in the face of international sanctions and sports boycotts. Censorship was stifling, with television only introduced in the 1970s. The stifling social atmosphere exacerbated political tensions.

Ever-growing internal resistance to, and international condemnation of, apartheid matched the steadfast resolution of the prisoners. The ANC's banning had driven it deep underground. Yet although the organization was now illegal—the state even made it illegal to display his photo or quote his writings—this could not stop the hundreds of thousands of people who had supported Congress from expressing their support in different ways.

With the ANC banned, new opposition forces emerged. Black Consciousness, led by charismatic student leader Steve Biko, took off in the late 1960s. Then in 1972–1973, the black labor movement came to life again in a sudden, massive strike wave. Things were on the boil and with a rigid, inflexible, and intolerant government at the helm of state, the country finally exploded in 1976, ignited by student protests in Soweto.

Although the 1976 protests were quashed by harsh measures from the state security forces that saw many casualties, popular resistance reemerged in the 1980s. This coalesced around vibrant, new mass organizations. The United Democratic Front (UDF, formed in 1983), was a very wide coalition of more than 600 community, labor, sport, and church organizations. The Congress of South African Trade Unions (COSATU, formed in 1985), with its largest affiliate, the National Union of Mineworkers (1982), led by ex-student activist Cyril Ramaphosa, grew rapidly and challenged the previously monolithic economic domination of the apartheid state. Many church leaders, such as Archbishop Desmond Tutu, lent their weight to popular protests. All across the country these diverse groups spoke out loudly and their support grew rapidly, with many people aligning themselves with the ideas of the ANC exemplified in the Freedom Charter. One of their major demands was the release of Mandela and all political prisoners.

Inspiration and hope also came to Mandela from overseas. The ANC saw four pillars to its struggle: mass-scale political action, the armed struggle, underground organization, and international solidarity. Increasingly, the latter force began to affect South Africa. Fellow Robben Island inmate Indres Naidoo recalls that the news that the names of their leaders such as Mandela and Sisulu were becoming famous internationally particularly cheered the prisoners.[26]

Around the world, the anti-apartheid movement became truly global, uniting student, church, labor, and political groups with specifically anti-apartheid organizations in which exiled South Africans often played a large part. Some governments, notably those in India, Scandinavia, and Eastern Europe, provided material aid to the ANC in exile. Many governments broadly implemented UN anti-apartheid resolutions, and more countries recognized the ANC than South Africa. However, it took decades to convince major Western powers, notably Britain and the United States and their transnational corporations, effectively to boycott Pretoria, which used many loopholes—trade in uranium, gold, arms, and oil, and "mercenary" sports teams—to try to boost its flagging status.

With some governments slow to act, the anti-apartheid movement developed its own forms of support, adopting "people's sanctions." Organizations such as the London-based International Defence and Aid Fund (IDAF) channeled valuable material resources to political prisoners, their families, and their lawyers; the work of IDAF, noted Mandela in 1992, was "absolutely vital" and a "morale booster."[27]

Also vital to the overall success of the movement of solidarity was the situation in the United States. Here there was a very broad range of anti-apartheid forces, such as the American Committee on Africa (which networked disinvestment campaigns), the Africa Fund (focusing on education and aid), the Congressional Black Caucus, TransAfrica, and the Free South African Movement, plus numerous federal and local labor, church, and student protest groups. This extensive movement created "new spaces in churches, campuses, stockholders meetings, entertainment and sports venues, city councils, and Congressional subcommittees to broaden support for the sanctions that bypassed state and corporate decision makers and exerted direct pressure on South Africa." If the American movement could ignite financial sanctions against the apartheid regime, then perhaps this would tip the balance in favor of change.[28]

By the 1980s, the anti-apartheid movements in many countries were able to coordinate global "weeks of protest." Many churches joined in. There were vigorous public boycotts of companies making money out of apartheid, notably oil giant Shell and those trading in South African products such as wine, fish, and gold kruggerand coins. More and more companies began to disinvest, some adopting "codes of conduct," such as the Sullivan Principles developed by the American businessperson Leon Sullivan, which, if they had limited effect, at least encouraged other corporations to divest.

At the same time, sporting sanctions hit the white South African community hard. This was particularly so when imposed by countries such as New Zealand and Australia, which shared tournaments of sports such as rugby that were popular among Afrikaners. More significantly, financial sanctions had a deep impact and helped modify the views of white South Africans. In particular, the U.S. Comprehensive Anti-Apartheid Act of 1986, which saw President Reagan's support for Pretoria finally overridden by Congress, and the refusal of U.S. banks to roll over South African loans, made sanctions a major force, eventually dragging Pretoria to the negotiating table.

A strong focus of this global anti-apartheid movement was the call for Nelson Mandela's release. By the 1980s, he had become a celebrated international prisoner of conscience and the most prominent opponent of apartheid. The British Commonwealth set up the Eminent Persons' Group, led by former Prime Ministers Malcolm Fraser of Australia and Olusegun Obasanjo of Nigeria. In February 1986, they met with Mandela in jail, who convinced them of his sincerity for peaceful change, but they also concluded that the South African government did not intend to negotiate in good faith.[29]

Throughout this period, many organizations bestowed upon Mandela numerous awards and honors, the number and status of which grew with time and added to pressure for his release. One of the first honors was as early as 1964, when the Students' Union of University College, London, elected him Honorary President. In 1973, a scientist who discovered a nuclear particle at the University of Leeds named it the Mandela Particle. India, the first country to impose sanctions on South Africa, awarded Mandela the Jawaharlal Nehru Award for International Understanding. By 1982, more than 2,000 mayors in 54 countries had signed a petition for his release. In 1983, the New York City square in front of South Africa's United Nations mission became "Nelson and Winnie Mandela Plaza." Numerous universities conferred honorary doctorates. A hit record in 1984 was "Free Nelson Mandela" by British pop group Special AKA. In the same year, the U.S. Senate approved a resolution calling for Mandela's release. Archbishop Trevor Huddleston, Mandela's old friend from Sophiatown and now leader of the British Anti-Apartheid Movement, presented on international petition of 50,000 signatures to the UN.

The anti-apartheid movement developed other effective techniques to expose apartheid; it built its own media with newsletters, cartoons, and posters. It adopted diverse tactics, including pickets, lobbying, consumer boycotts, industrial action, sports disruption, mass rallies, and concerts. In 1988, many worldwide events commemorated Mandela's 70th birthday: in June, a massive crowd of 72,000 packed Wembley Stadium in London for a rock concert, singing and chanting "Free Nelson Mandela" along with a galaxy of world artists including Whitney Houston and Harry Belafonte. Winnie Mandela sent a message, saying it had given South Africans renewed hope that "the whole world is with us in our struggle." Ahmed Kathrada, still in jail, mused in a letter to friends that apart from Christmas, he could not recall "any person in history whose birthday has been so widely celebrated as Nelson's." Popular anti-apartheid feature films such as *Cry Freedom* and several documentaries on Mandela raised consciousness about apartheid and his fate. Writers, artists, cartoonists, and musicians from Bob Marley to Stevie Wonder inspired thousands of youth with their anti-apartheid lyrics. Star performers, massive rock concerts, and public debate helped sway the global mass media, which almost nightly featured TV pictures of police dogs and *sjambok* whips tearing into defenseless people in South African streets, finally destroying the apartheid regime's last shreds of credibility.[30]

By the late 1980s, therefore, widespread global protests had thoroughly tainted apartheid South Africa with international pariah status, resulting in international sanctions and disinvestment that destabilized the economy and disrupted the regime's tight hold on power.

In the meantime, MK, the military wing that Mandela had founded, continued to operate from exile in the nearby African "front line states," which the South African government repeatedly tried to destabilize with military attacks and "dirty tricks." South African spies assassinated Mandela's old friend, the Jewish journalist Ruth First, with a parcel bomb sent to her office in neighboring Mozambique. MK forces were relatively small and poorly armed, but they provided a concrete symbol of resistance. Word of their exploits reaching the prisoners lifted their spirits: "We were very excited," wrote Mandela, to see MK grow into a people's army and attack strongholds of the apartheid regime such as the oil refinery Sasol.[31]

With all this turbulence and with international sanctions starting to bite, sectors of white South African society became willing to negotiate. White businesspeople began to visit African countries such as Zambia and Senegal for preliminary talks with the ANC in exile, which had become a virtual government-in-waiting. Inside his prison walls, Mandela increasingly resembled a president-in-waiting.

By the mid-1980s, Mandela occupied a rather odd position; the government would not release him, yet without him, they could not hope to resolve the deep political-economic crises wracking the country. There were moves to test his willingness to accept a conditional release; his relative Kaiser Matanzima, now an open accomplice of the apartheid system as a Bantustan chief, offered to host Mandela in the Transkei if he stayed there, out of the way. Mandela refused on principle. In February 1985, South African President P. W. Botha offered conditional release if Mandela renounced violence. Mandela retorted that only free persons can negotiate, and reminded Botha that he still had not even accorded him the status of political prisoner. Mandela's daughter Zindzi read a defiant and moving message from her father to a packed crowd in Orlando Football Stadium in Soweto in which he refused to separate his freedom from that of his people.

> I cannot sell my birthright, nor am I prepared to sell the birthright of the people to be free. . . . What freedom am I being offered while the organization of the people remains banned? . . . What freedom am I being offered to live my life . . . with my dear wife who remains in banishment? . . . I cannot and will not give any undertaking at a time when I and you, the people, are not free. Your freedom and mine cannot be separated. . . . Only free men can negotiate. Prisoners cannot. . . . I will return.[32]

Despite this deadlock, there were subtle signs of change. The nature of Mandela's prison accommodation had been changing for the better. In 1982, the government had moved him and other key leaders from Robben Island to Pollsmoor Prison on the mainland near Cape Town. In 1985, he was isolated even from these close friends, given three rooms on a different floor, and largely prevented from speaking to them.

This separation from the other prisoners and the resultant solitude led Mandela to decide that he now had an opportunity to initiate secret talks with the government. These he began tentatively in 1985, and they gathered pace in 1988, but at first led nowhere mainly because the dogmatic P. W. Botha remained in power. Botha pulled back from an excellent opportunity for compromise, instead launching destabilizing military attacks on neighboring countries and maintaining a state of emergency inside South Africa that tolerated no real freedom of dissent.

Mandela therefore remained a prisoner as the years dragged on. In 1988, he contracted tuberculosis, and authorities in December of that year transferred him once more, this time to Victor Verster Prison near the town of Paarl, 40 minutes northeast of Cape Town. All of a sudden, Mandela was in very different surroundings: a warden's bungalow complete with "royal trimmings" such as thick carpets and expensive furniture, white wardens acting virtually as servants, bodyguards, a swimming pool, and a fax machine. Yet "stripped of all these fineries," observed Kathrada at the time, Mandela was "still a prisoner."[33]

In trying to find a negotiated solution, Mandela was in a difficult, complex position. There was political stalemate with neither side able to defeat the other, so he had decided it was time to press for negotiations, but only if the government was willing to renounce violence, free political prisoners, lift the ban on the ANC, and permit open political activity. At first, he still was cut off from both the internal anti-apartheid resistance and the ANC in exile, and therefore unable properly to consult with them. It was, noted biographer Anthony Sampson, "the loneliest stretch in Mandela's ordeal." At first his close comrades—Sisulu and Kathrada—were skeptical of talks, with Oliver Tambo in exile and the UDF inside the country even more so, concerned that the government might be manipulating him. Yet, they appreciated that, given Mandela's stubbornness, they could hardly stop him. Gradually, however, he was allowed to contact the ANC and became more accessible; for his birthday in July 1989, he was able to have a full family reunion as well as a meeting with Sisulu and Kathrada.[34]

Mandela put his whole life's reputation clearly on the line in agreeing to talk to a regime still launching bloody assaults on its own people and still regarded internationally as a pariah state. It was a bold, seemingly risky, move. In March 1989, Mandela drew up a detailed memorandum to try to break the political bottleneck. Botha had suffered a stroke and had begun to withdraw from official duties, but finally met Mandela in July. The talks were inconclusive and the following month Botha resigned as president, replaced by F. W. de Klerk, previously a hard-line supporter of apartheid, but starting to show signs of compromise. In August, the ANC in exile and its supporters adopted the Harare Declaration, which while remaining firm to its historic principles, opened the door to a negotiated settlement. Mandela had seen and approved the document in advance, and inside the country UDF structures, now organized as the Mass Democratic Movement, supported the move. De Klerk and Mandela finally met in December 1989 amid rumors of his possible release; his old Robben Island friends, Sisulu and Kathrada, had already left prison in October.

The experience of trials and prison made Mandela even more concerned with unity. His incarceration for 27 long years had important political effects, most notably preventing ANC leaders from negotiating with a government that became increasingly extreme in its policies. On the other hand, by bringing the anti-apartheid leaders together, jail experience ironically enhanced their unity and dedication to their ideals. Nevertheless, although Mandela and his comrades never wavered in their unwillingness to compromise over the evil of apartheid, the long years of imprisonment served to blunt some of their earlier, more radical social goals and to some extent distanced them from those inside the country committed to changing the entire political and economic system upon which apartheid rested.

Any form of imprisonment, of course, aims to stifle prisoner rebelliousness, and Mandela was well aware of its impact. Eddie Daniels, when he met Mandela briefly outside Pollsmoor, remarked how beautiful the prison looked from the outside, with its flowers. Mandela shot back: "Danie, a prison is like a grave, beautiful outside but with decaying humanity inside." However, as Daniels points out, Mandela was *always* a person open to compromise. Mandela used his great diplomatic and human skills not only to unify the movement but also to chart an alternative, negotiated route out of the chaos and violence that ever more enveloped South Africa in the 1980s.[35]

Despite the traumas of 27 years in prison, Nelson Mandela maintained his commitment to principle; he refused freedom if other political prisoners remained in jail, or if the ANC and its allies remained banned; democracy had to come. By 1989, he was in close touch with not only the government but also the ANC exile leadership and the ANC underground. Mandela and other ANC leaders could finally see some kind of change on the way; the endgame of apartheid was beginning, but it would be an unknown, difficult, and perilous final path to freedom.[36]

NOTES

1. Ahmed Kathrada, *Letters from Robben Island: A Selection of Ahmed Kathrada's Prison Correspondence, 1964–1989*, edited by Robert Vassen (East Lansing, MI: Michigan State University Press, 1999), p. 65; Padraig O'Malley, *Shades of Difference: Mac Maharaj and the Struggle for South Africa* (New York: Viking, 2007), p. 148.

2. Nelson Mandela, *Long Walk to Freedom: The Autobiography of Nelson Mandela* (Boston: Little, Brown, 1994), p. 353.

3. Mandela, *Long Walk to Freedom*, pp. 334–338; Maharaj interview in O'Malley, *Shades of Difference*, p. 160; Walter Sisulu interview with John Carlin, 1999, in *The Long Walk of Nelson Mandela*: http://www.pbs.org/wgbh/pages/front line/shows/mandela/interviews/sisulu.html.

4. Helen Suzman, *In No Uncertain Terms: A South African Memoir* (New York: Knopf, 1993), pp. 150–151; Mandela, *Long Walk to Freedom*, pp. 380–381.

5. Fran Lisa Buntman, *Robben Island and Prisoner Resistance to Apartheid* (New York: Cambridge University Press, 2003); Noel Solani and Noor Nieftagodien, "Political Imprisonment and Resistance on Robben Island: The Case of Robben Island, 1960–1970," in *The Road to Democracy in South Africa*, pp. 391–410.

6. Nelson Mandela, Foreword to O'Malley, *Shades of Difference*, pp. 1, 4.

7. Letter of Mandela to Fatima Meer, cited in Fatima Meer, *Higher than Hope: The Authorized Biography of Nelson Mandela* (New York: Harper, 1990), p. 269.

8. Eddie Daniels, interview with the author, October 13, 2006, East Lansing, MI; Eddie Daniels, *There and Back: Robben Island 1964–1979* (Cape Town: Mayibuye Books, 1998), pp. 196–201.

9. Eddie Daniels, interview with the author.

10. Michael Dingake, *My Fight against Apartheid* (London: Kliptown Books, 1987), pp. 213–224.

11. Eddie Daniels, interview with the author; Mac Mahararj, editor, *Reflections in Prison* (Cape Town: Robben Island Museum, 2001), p. 5; Mandela, *Long Walk to Freedom*, p. 365.

12. Mandela, *Long Walk to Freedom*, p. 374; Interview with Govan Mbeki by John Carlin; Tom Lodge, *Mandela: A Critical Life* (New York: Oxford University Press, 2006), p. 133.

13. Mandela, *Long Walk to Freedom*, pp. 366–368; Mahararj, *Reflections in Prison*, p.7.

14. Mandela, *Long Walk to Freedom*, p. 361; Eddie Daniels, interview with the author; *Letters from Robben Island*, pp. 70, 150, and letter of Ahmed Kathrada to Solly Kathrada, August 30, 1969, Kathrada Collection, Michigan State University Library, p. 150.

15. Kathrada to Tom Vassen, November 22, 1975, in *Letters from Robben Island*, p. 76.

16. Cited in Isabel Hofmeyr, "Reading Debating/Debating Reading: The Case of the Lovedale Literary Society, or Why Mandela Quotes Shakespeare," in Karin Barber, ed., *Africa's Hidden Histories: Everyday Literacy and Making the Self* (Bloomington: Indiana University Press, 2006), pp. 258–277, p. 259; Ahmed Kathrada letter to Sonia Bunting, London, February 16, 1975, in *Letters from Robben Island*, p. 64.

17. Eddie Daniels, interview with the author.

18. Mandela, *Long Walk to Freedom*, p. 351; Meer, *Higher Than Hope*, p. 344. The absurdity of the prison censors was seen in their objection to Kathrada's mild criticism in a letter of the quality of the Tarzan and Dracula films they had to endure: Ahmed Kathrada to Shireen Patel, June 19, 1976, Kathrada Collection, Michigan State University Library.

19. Meer, *Higher Than Hope*, pp. 337–339; Winnie Mandela, *Part of My Soul* (New York: Viking Penguin, 1985), p. 137.

20. Mandela letter to his daughters, June 1, 1970, in *A Prisoner in the Garden*, p. 101; Ahmed Kathrada, public lecture, Michigan State University Museum, March 19, 2006.

21. Benjamin Pogrund, *War of Words: Memoirs of a South African Journalist* (New York: Seven Stories Press, 2000), p. 318.

22. Winnie Mandela, *Part of My Soul*, pp. 24, 31–39.

23. Winnie Mandela interview with Peter Davis, Brandfort, June 27, 1985, Peter Davis Collection; *Winnie Mandela Interview Unedited* (Vancouver: Villon Films, 1985). Anti-apartheid activists often developed close personal relationships with each other. In 1962, with Mandela banned, Kathrada drove all the way to Swaziland to fetch Mandela's children, whom the Mother Superior only released into his care when they joyously recognized him as part of their extended family: Ahmed Kathrada to Zohra Kathrada, June 12, 1988, *Letters from Robben Island*, p. 229.

24. Gilbey, *The Lady*, chapters 9–10; Lodge, *Mandela: A Critical Life*, p. 183.

25. Winnie Mandela, *Part of My Soul*, p. 130; "Mandela: An Audio History": http://www.radiodiaries.org/mandela/mpeople.html.

26. Indres Naidoo, *Robben Island: Ten Years as a Political Prisoner in South Africa's Most Notorious Penitentiary* (New York: Vintage, 1983), p. 189.

27. Denis Herbstein, *White Lies: Canon Collins and the Secret War against Apartheid* (Cape Town: HSRC Press, 2004), p. 328.

28. Donald Culverson, *Contesting Apartheid: U.S. Activism, 1960–1987* (Boulder, CO: Westview, 1999), pp. 157–159; Francis Njubi Nesbitt, *Race for Sanctions: African Americans against Apartheid, 1946–1994* (Bloomington: Indiana University Press, 2004); Håkan Thörn, *Anti-Apartheid and the Emergence of a Global Civil Society* (New York: Palgrave, 2006). See also online resources: http://www.anc.org.za/ancdocs/history/aam/.

29. Record of discussions with Mandela, February 1986, Malcolm Fraser Papers, University of Melbourne Archives; telephone interview by the author with Malcolm Fraser, 26 March 2006.

30. *Free Nelson Mandela: Festival Concert Book* (New York: Penguin, 1988), pp. 8–9; Ahmed Kathrada to Bob and Tom Vassen, August 28, 1988, Kathrada Collection.

31. "Umkhonto's First Commander" (interview with Mandela) in *Submit or Fight! 30 Years of Umkhonto we Sizwe* (Johannesburg: ANC, 1991), pp. 6–9.

32. Mandela, Sisulu, Mhalaba, Kathrada, and Mlangeni to Botha, February 13, 1985, in *Letters from Robben Island*, pp. 168–173; Mandela, "I Am Not Prepared to Sell the Birthright of the People to Be Free": http://www.anc.org.za/ancdocs/history/mandela/64–90/jabulani.html.

33. Letter of Kathrada to Marie Kola, July 19, 1989, in *Letters from Robben Island*, p. 258.

34. Mandela, *Long Walk to Freedom*, p. 457; Elinor Sisulu, *Walter and Albertina Sisulu: In Our Lifetime* (Cape Town: D. Philip, 2002), pp. 352–355; Anthony Sampson, *Mandela: The Authorized Biography* (New York: Knopf, 1999), pp. 364, 376–379, 387; Lodge, *Mandela: A Critical Life*, p. 160.

35. Eddie Daniels, interview with the author.

36. Elias Maluleke, "Mandela: Can He Save South Africa?" *Pace*, March 1990, p. 6.

Chapter 8

FREE AT LAST: RELEASE AND TRANSITION TO DEMOCRACY

Free at last! Widespread public manifestations of joy and hope swept the country on Nelson Mandela's release from captivity on February 11, 1990. As he walked hand in hand with Winnie through the gates of Victor Verster prison, he realized that his "ten thousand days of imprisonment" had ended. Amidst a sea of supporters and media, Mandela raised his right fist and the crowd responded with a roar. "I had not been able to do that for twenty-seven years and it gave me a surge of strength and joy. . . . As I finally walked through those gates . . . I felt even at the age of seventy-one that my life was beginning anew."[1]

In the final years of his imprisonment, Mandela had entered into a hesitant dialogue with apartheid leaders, but he had rejected any conditional release that ignored the democratic rights of his people. Now, ongoing economic and political crises inside South Africa interacted with deep-seated global and regional changes to incline the apartheid regime to risk his release.

The South African economy was under enormous strain following the application of international financial sanctions and given the ongoing political instability inside the country. The growing economic effects of globalization made conflict resolution imperative if the crisis-ridden economy was to stabilize. Internal dissent was on the rise.

A major factor changing the geopolitics of the region was the independence in 1990 of the neighboring country of Namibia, which South Africa had occupied since World War I, and later even in defiance of United Nations resolutions. This had been hastened by South African military defeat in Angola at the hands of Cuba. Even more significant was the end of the Cold War, which removed many obstacles to negotiations. The collapse of the socialist bloc in Eastern Europe meant that the ruling National Party could no longer use the specter of communism as an excuse not to negotiate, and for its part, the ANC now lacked a major material base to continue its armed struggle. As these events transpired, in retrospect Mandela's decision to open negotiations seemed far-sighted.

On February 2, President F. W. de Klerk had surprised many people by announcing at the opening of Parliament the unbanning of the ANC and other illegal political parties and the release of some political prisoners. He also foreshadowed a degree of political reform by scrapping some pillars of apartheid such as the Separate Amenities Act.

All eyes were on Mandela to see if he could do what others had found impossible: end apartheid and bring peace to the troubled country. Everywhere he received a hero's welcome. Mandela immediately assumed leadership of the democratic movement. He also toured the world to thank many countries and their peoples for their solidarity. Over the next four years, Mandela would lead the thrust towards a transition to democracy, a complicated process at a time of great political conflict in which his diplomatic and tactical skills would be crucial. A new phase of South African history was opening.

On the evening of February 11, 1990, Mandela returned to Cape Town to give a remarkable address from a balcony overlooking the vast Parade ground where hundreds of thousands of well-wishers thronged. He was both optimistic, declaring his faith in open negotiations to spark a genuine political transition to democracy, and cautious, urging vigilance. He conceded that F. W. de Klerk had gone further than any other apartheid leader, but warned of dangers ahead and pointed out that peace was impossible without free political activity and the release of *all* political prisoners. Mandela appropriately and symbolically ended the speech with the same words he had spoken before going to prison 27 years earlier: he was prepared to struggle and if need be die to achieve a democratic and free society with equal opportunities for all.[2]

Two days later, Mandela returned to his home in Soweto. He addressed a huge rally at Orlando Football Stadium. The massive welcome visibly touched him; it filled "my heart with joy." Yet, he was saddened to learn of continued black suffering. He urged children to return to school, reiterating the message of his open letter to the press sent while still in prison on January 27, 1990, in which he called on youth "to arm themselves with the most powerful weapons of modern times—education, and education."[3]

Mandela threw himself into political work with the energy of a young man as the ANC quickly and effectively reestablished its structures inside the country. He also strode the world stage like a colossus. In March 1990, he traveled to Lusaka, Zambia to meet the ANC's exiled leadership and then to Sweden to meet ANC President Oliver Tambo, recovering from a heart stroke. Mandela would replace Tambo as ANC leader the following year. In coming months, Mandela would travel the globe raising funds, but increased tension and the prospect of negotiations soon compelled him to return home.

President De Klerk argues that initially he had known little of the secret government negotiations with Mandela, but gradually as he assumed power he become convinced, both by events and by his own religious calling, that he had to abandon the old racist dogmas of apartheid that he too had supported. His relationship with Mandela over the next four years would be complex, and at times sharp, but would be an important factor in determining the nature and rate of change.[4]

As the ANC and the government came to the negotiating table, a new stage of the anti-apartheid struggle, one that was different and in some ways more difficult than before, now opened. Mandela was flexible on methods, but resolute on principle, and the enormous pressure for change from below helped him maintain this commitment. He was under pressure from all sides—white business wanted assurances against nationalization of their wealth; black labor wanted a fair redistribution of the national wealth always denied Africans.

In this unfolding drama, Mandela would not be alone—a multitude of skilled people from within the ranks of the ANC and the broad democratic movement joined him in negotiations—but he would play the crucial role. If in the confines of the cold and windswept Robben Island, Mandela had unified the prisoners, then since 1985 five years of delicate, secret talks with government, prolonged debates with fellow prisoners over strategy and tactics, and his solitude all honed his negotiating skills. He would need such skills, for democracy in South Africa did not emerge spontaneously; rather, many people of goodwill built it laboriously in a protracted process that was accompanied by chronic violence as powerful, vested interests resisted change.

Things at first moved fast. At the end of April 1990, the first official group of ANC leaders returned from exile. The forces of the ANC now merged with those of UDF to form an experienced negotiating team, led by Mandela. Three days of talks early in May produced the Groote Schuur Accord, in which the governing National Party and the ANC committed to a process of negotiations and reduction of tension. In August, the

Pretoria Minute, a written agreement between the government and the ANC, formalized further release of political prisoners by the state, while the ANC unilaterally agreed to suspend all armed actions.

Unfortunately, serious political conflict would soon create roadblocks on the road to negotiations for a new constitution. Terrible political violence wracked neighborhoods in some parts of the country. Many commentators accused the government, or at least a covert "third force," of orchestrating internecine violence between the ANC and the conservative Inkatha Freedom Party led by Mangosuthu Buthelezi, a paid official of the government's Bantustan system. In June 1991, the "Inkathagate Scandal" revealed army involvement in secret political death squads, tarnishing the reputation of De Klerk and Buthelezi, and prompting Mandela and the ANC to suspend bilateral meetings. The findings of the subsequent Goldstone Commission into political violence largely confirmed Mandela's misgivings about this mysterious "third force."

Nevertheless, Mandela and his leadership team pushed ahead, calling in July 1991 for the installation of an Interim Government. Mandela went into overdrive, urging peace: at one political rally in Natal, he risked raising the ire of his own supporters by urging them to abandon violence and throw their weapons into the sea. In September, he signed an important milestone, the National Peace Accord. However, discussions would remain protracted, with disagreements and periodic breakdown of talks.[5]

Multiparty negotiations now took the form of the Convention for a Democratic South Africa (CODESA), a forum to negotiate a new constitution. Employing the notion of "sufficient consensus" to reach decisions, CODESA's first meeting in December 1991 adopted a Declaration of Intent signed by all major political parties except the Inkatha Freedom Party and the Bophuthatswana government. De Klerk, speaking last, apologized for apartheid policies but prevaricated on one person-one vote, insisting on special minority rights for whites through power sharing. De Klerk then questioned the ANC's commitment to peace, urging the disbanding of its armed wing, MK. Mandela was furious and demanded the right of reply, condemning De Klerk for trying to torpedo change and arguing that only with an Interim Government could the people, facing murderous political violence, renounce their self-defense units.

The question of armed self-defense was an important one for Mandela at this time. The ANC was not willing to risk everything when many signs pointed to continuing danger. There were strong rumors of a coup by the army, many of whose leaders opposed De Klerk's moves toward democracy. Buthelezi launched a violent campaign against the ANC, exploiting loopholes in customary law that allowed his followers to carry "traditional weapons" that nevertheless could, and did, inflict serious harm. Although the very fact of Mandela's release and the start of negotiations had spawned metaphors of a "small miracle" and the birth of a "new South Africa," history suggested to many people a more pessimistic outcome. In this context, Mandela gave his blessing to his old Robben Island companion Mac Maharaj to strengthen MK underground structures inside the country through a campaign entitled Operation Vula. Maharaj eventually was arrested, but the ANC had shown that it could mount large-scale support backed by smuggled arms, and this acted as somewhat of a brake on those seeking to resort to a military coup.[6]

Mandela played a pivotal role at this time, moderating ANC radicals but holding the government to the need for real change and an end to political violence. In February 1992, De Klerk accepted the ANC demand for an Interim Government, but a sticking point remained general constitutional principles. De Klerk faced strong opposition to change from far-right extremist Afrikaners wanting to retain their race-based privileges. Therefore, in March, but without consulting Mandela, he called a whites-only referendum, winning 67 percent support for his broad reforms.

Negotiations continued around deciding a process toward democracy. There was general agreement around a Transitional Executive Council to prepare elections for an interim government and constituent assembly, but the second CODESA meeting in May 1992 deadlocked around the size of the majority needed to approve a new constitution. Then, a terrible massacre by pro-Inkatha armed hostel dwellers—with rumors of state involvement—of dozens of residents at Boipatong township in June 1992 saw Mandela accuse the regime of complicity and break off negotiations. De Klerk would still not agree to simple majority rule, but he eventually disbanded three security battalions suspected of covert terror and agreed to international monitoring of the conflict.

The political pendulum now swung back and forth. The ANC and its allies, the powerful COSATU labor federation and the South African Communist Party (SACP, also legalized in 1990), now called the Tripartite Alliance, launched a campaign of rolling protests. Such popular pressure helped bring the parties together again, and a September 1992 summit meeting agreed on a Record of Understanding around constitutional change, political prisoners, and conflict resolution. In the same month, however, serious violence again erupted, in Bisho, capital of the Ciskei Bantustan, where police opened fire on protesters, the massacre again delaying negotiations.

Mandela and his negotiating team persisted despite all these interruptions and provocations. In particular, he showed his willingness to compromise at times of crisis. In November 1992, negotiations resumed. Once again, violence intervened, this time nearly derailing the talks. The assassination of the charismatic and highly popular ANC and SACP leader Chris Hani in April 1993 by a right-wing terrorist created an explosive situation only defused by Mandela's appeal for calm on national television. His timely intervention was facilitated by De Klerk, who, isolated in the rural areas at the time, sensed "this was Mandela's moment, not mine." Afterwards, Mandela needed all his tact when a mourning crowd in Soweto, still enraged at the murder, booed his call for peace.[7]

Talks resumed, now in the form of the Multi-Party Negotiating Forum to address the mechanics of a transition process. There was not, however, a complete consensus. Mandela's old rivals, the Pan Africanist Congress and their allies the Azanian People's Organization boycotted the talks, as did the Conservative Party, an Afrikaner break-away from De Klerk's National Party. The final obstacles to peace would be from the Afrikaner far right wing and Inkatha, in a few last, desperate efforts to stave off the triumph of democracy.

In June 1993, far right-wing extremist vigilantes used vehicles to ram the building where talks were underway but did not prevent agreement opening the way to elections. De Klerk now dropped demands for white minority rights. In November 1993, negotiators agreed an interim constitution legalizing elections to establish a Government of National Unity, and, in January 1994, a power-sharing Transitional Executive Council to oversee elections emerged.

Mandela still had much work to do. Ultraconservative Afrikaners led by army General Constand Viljoen began to mobilize around the idea of a self-governing Afrikaner *volkstaat* (homeland). In March 1994, they launched an abortive military action in the Bophuthatswana Bantustan. The complete failure of the adventure stimulated popular discontent that saw Bophuthatswana completely collapse, to be reincorporated into South Africa. Mandela intervened to guarantee Bophuthatswana civil servants their jobs in a future united South Africa. A crisis in another disintegrating Bantustan, Ciskei, saw it also reincorporated: the apartheid dream of a racially divided constellation of quiescent black ministates was over. Abandoning military intervention, Viljoen formed a legal party and, strongly encouraged by Mandela, agreed to contest the elections. Inkatha, which had withdrawn from talks, at the last minute agreed to take part in the election. Mandela had worked hard to allay the fears of all parties: for example, media images of him drinking tea with the aging widow of Verwoerd, the architect of apartheid, helped assure

Afrikaners that political change could accommodate their own culture and interests.

Neither did Mandela ignore the important international dimensions of ending apartheid. From 1990, he toured widely, thanking countries for their support and gathering much-needed funds for the ANC's future electoral needs. Once initial negotiations were agreed upon, in June 1990 he headed off on a six-week tour of Europe, the United Kingdom, North America, and Africa, everywhere greeted with acclaim and honors by heads of state. Hundreds of thousands of people lined the streets, as in New York City and Detroit, where he addressed huge crowds at Yankee and Tiger Stadiums respectively. The U.S. Congress gave him a standing ovation. In Harlem, he attended the Canaan Baptist Church to pay tribute together with Jesse Jackson to all the American churches that had supported the anti-apartheid struggle.[8]

Later in 1990, Mandela visited Norway, Zambia, India, and Australia, and in 1991 West Africa and South America. In December he met U.S. President George H. W. Bush. In the same month, Mandela addressed the United Nations General Assembly in New York, urging continued sanctions until free elections occurred.

Eager to open up space for negotiations, the ANC initially encouraged the partial lifting of sports sanctions but continued to lobby against premature lifting of economic sanctions, worried that change could easily still be derailed. However, in September 1993, while visiting the United States, Mandela articulated a change of strategy, now urging the lifting of economic sanctions. To encourage investment, he signaled that the ANC's Freedom Charter policy of nationalization was only one possible policy option.

The grueling schedule of overseas trips was important to raise funds for the cash-strapped ANC, banned for three decades. However, sometimes there were dilemmas in accepting money. Mandela received generous donations both from Indonesian military dictator Suharto, who had imposed massive human rights violations on the people of his own country and those of East Timor, and from Nigeria's Abacha dictatorship. On the other hand, those countries had been opponents of apartheid, as had many other states including Cuba and Libya, which Mandela continued to treat as friendly because of their solidarity. He found subtle ways to encourage conflict resolution: in September 1994, he urged Suharto to open dialogue with East Timorese resistance leaders and later met with resistance leader Xanana Gusmão.

For the transition to democracy to succeed, there was a need for compromise and social reconciliation. There were glimpses of hope. Despite clear tensions—Mandela had seriously questioned De Klerk's integrity and held him partly responsible for savage attacks on ANC supporters—in 1993 the two men jointly received the Nobel Peace Prize "for their work for the peaceful termination of the apartheid regime, and for laying the foundations for a new democratic South Africa." In his acceptance speech, Mandela praised De Klerk for having had "the courage to admit that a terrible wrong had been done to our country and people." He paid tribute to previous Nobel Laureates, Albert Luthuli, Desmond Tutu, and Martin Luther King. He also spoke "as a representative of the millions of people across the globe, the anti-apartheid movement, the governments, and organizations" that had opposed apartheid. Mindful that international solidarity had contributed to his release, he reminded listeners that solidarity must continue, not just to ensure the final burying of apartheid but also to free another Nobel laureate, Aung San Suu Kyi of Burma.[9]

Despite these triumphs, there was personal pain. Although the dedicated support of family and friends had made the lonely years of prison easier, new political obligations rent Mandela's marriage asunder. In April 1992, he called a press conference to announce a separation, followed four years later by divorce. The breakup was painful on all sides. Some of Mandela's peers saw Winnie as a political "loose canon," and their pressure, notes fellow Robben Island veteran Fikile Bam, also moved Mandela to place national interests first. Family friend Fatima Meer blamed the media but observed that Mandela as chief negotiator felt obliged to support "law and order" in the face of serious charges against Winnie over the 1989 events involving her Mandela Football Club gang. Mandela captured the dilemmas he constantly faced in balancing politics with family interests when recounting that his daughter Zindzi had felt that, after growing up without a father, she finally saw him return only to then become "father of the nation" instead.[10]

Public attention now swung to elections. Could the ANC receive enough votes to govern in its own right? As Mandela sat in endless negotiating meetings, he realized the great disadvantage the ANC faced relative to the well-established and well-funded National Party of De Klerk. More than seventeen million Africans had never voted, and most lived in rural areas, with illiteracy as high as 67 percent.[11] Mandela continued to campaign tirelessly for the elections. He stood firm against Buthelezi, who wanted the elections delayed but who, at the very last minute, agreed to participate.

Nelson Mandela's role in this transition period was vital. He united and mobilized Africans and their allies as never before. On the world stage, he became a much-admired celebrity who accrued enormous respect, goodwill, and support.[12] Of course, Mandela would be the first to argue that many other individuals and organizations also were instrumental in this historical process. De Klerk broke the logjam of rigid Afrikaner politics. A range of remarkable personalities, such as Archbishop Tutu and other church leaders like Beyers Naudé, and ANC and National Party leaders such as Cyril Ramaphosa and Rolf Meyer, Thabo Mbeki, and Joe Slovo were firmly behind the peace process. In addition, hundreds of thousands of ordinary South Africans had had enough of violence and racism, and through their attendance at countless rallies they "voted with their feet" in favor of democracy. Yet, it was Mandela who had initiated and then driven this process to its conclusion, providing inspired leadership at every turn.

It had indeed been a "long walk to freedom," and Mandela anxiously but optimistically awaited the outcome of the election.

NOTES

1. Nelson Mandela, *Long Walk to Freedom. The Autobiography of Nelson Mandela* (Boston: Little, Brown, 1994), p. 491.

2. To hear the speech see *Mandela: Free at Last* (Globalvision, 1990) or *Mandela: An Audio History* Part 5: Democracy (1990–94): http://www.radiodiaries.org/mandela/mstories.html.

3. Elias Maluleke, "Mandela: Can He Save South Africa?" *Pace*, March 1990, p. 16.

4. Allister Sparks, *Tomorrow Is Another Country: The Inside Story of South Africa's Negotiated Revolution* (New York: Hill and Wang, 1995).

5. Perceptive accounts of the transition include Sparks, *Tomorrow is Another Country*, and Patti Waldmeir, *Anatomy of a Miracle* (New York: Viking, 1997).

6. Conny Braam, *Operation Vula* (Belleville, South Africa: Jacana, 2004).

7. F. W. de Klerk, *The Last Trek: A New Beginning: The Autobiography* (London: Macmillan, 1998), p. 276.

8. Francis Njubi Nesbitt, *Race for Sanctions: African Americans against Apartheid, 1946–1994* (Bloomington: Indiana University Press, 2004), p. 162; Robert K. Massie, *Loosing the Bonds: The United States and South Africa in the Apartheid Years* (New York: Doubleday, 1997), p. 666.

9. For online details see: nobelprize.org/nobel_prizes/peace/laureates/1993.

10. Fatima Meer and Fikile Bam interviewed by John Carlin, 1999, in *The Long Walk of Nelson Mandela*: http://www.pbs.org/wgbh/pages/frontline/shows/mandela/interviews.

11. Facsimile extract from Mandela's handwritten CODESA notes, reproduced in *A Prisoner in the Garden* (New York: Viking Studio, 2006), p. 49.

12. See James Barber, *Mandela's World: The International Dimension of South Africa's Political Revolution 1990–99* (Athens: Ohio University Press, 2004).

Chapter 9

PRESIDENCY AND NEW CHALLENGES

On April 27, 1994, South Africans stood in snaking queues around the country as millions of Africans, many of them elderly, voted for the first time in their lives. There had been last-minute hitches: only at the very last minute had the conservative Inkatha Freedom Party agreed to take part in the election, and ballot papers had to have its emblem glued on top. Prospects for peace in the conflict-wracked province of Natal dominated by Inkatha's rural power base still seemed dim, and Nelson Mandela decided to go there himself to cast his own vote as a way of showing the people it was safe to vote.

It was a poignant moment, full of historic symbolism. Mandela chose to vote at Ohlange School, not far from the grave of John Dube. Educated in the African American Tuskegee College, Dube in 1912 had become founder-president of the ANC. Dube's mission of unity and nonracialism, mused Mandela, was about to be fulfilled. Across the verdant valley lay the settlement of Phoenix, where Mahatma Gandhi's printing press had proclaimed similarly the need for racial and political tolerance. At the age of 76, Mandela voted in a national election for the first time ever. The denial to Africans of such a basic human right as the vote had underpinned the very fabric of colonialism and then apartheid, but Mandela was determined to make a fresh start.

The result was a landslide victory to Mandela and the ANC, with 62.6 percent of the vote. This was just short of the two-thirds required for the ANC to change the constitution on its own, but Mandela was pleased in the sense that the need for cooperation with other political parties would strengthen multiparty democracy. Despite a bad case of influenza, he joined the celebrations. Among foreign dignitaries present was Coretta Scott King, widow of Martin Luther King Jr. In his address Mandela, looking directly at her, invoked the memory of her late husband. His comments captured the significance of the historic day:

> This is one of the most important moments in the life of our country. I stand here before you filled with deep pride and joy—pride in the ordinary, humble people of this country. You have shown such a calm, patient determination to reclaim this country as your own, and now the joy that we can loudly proclaim from the rooftops—Free at last! Free at last! . . . This is a time to heal the old wounds and build a new South Africa.[1]

The country went crazy with joy. There were wild celebrations in the black townships; even the once repressive police joined in, honking their car horns. South Africa was indeed "Free At Last," reported the *New York Times*.[2]

On May 9, the first session of the new National Assembly elected Mandela unopposed as president of South Africa. The next day was his presidential inauguration at the Union Buildings in the capital, Pretoria. Among the 4,000 guests were anti-apartheid activists from around the world and even some of Mandela's prison warders. An unusually varied cross-section of foreign visitors was present, ranging from U.S. government representatives Vice President Al Gore and First Lady Hillary Clinton, to Fidel Castro, Israeli President Chaim Hertzog, and the Palestine Liberation Organization's Yasser Arafat, and numerous African leaders such as Julius Nyerere, together with Prince Charles of England. It was testimony to the breadth not only of ANC diplomatic ties but also of Mandela's aura. His inauguration speech was short but inspirational. He concluded by stating, "Let there be justice for all. Let there be peace for all. Let there be work, bread, water and salt for all. . . . Never, never and never again shall it be that this beautiful land will again experience the oppression of one by another and suffer the indignity of being the skunk of the world. Let freedom reign."[3]

Later in the year Mandela's autobiography, *Long Walk to Freedom*, which many years earlier had been smuggled out of prison by Mac Maharaj, broke all South African book sale records. Mandela concluded the book by emphasizing the huge task ahead to bring reconciliation to a nation deeply divided by race hatred. All people, he reasoned, including the oppressor, needed liberating, and South Africans had only taken the first step to freedom on a long, difficult road to respect the rights of all: "I have walked that long road to freedom. . . . But I can rest only for a moment, for with freedom comes responsibilities, and I dare not linger, for my long walk is not yet ended."[4]

Over the next five years, Mandela and his government would go a very long way toward laying the groundwork for such reconciliation. In large part this would be due to his own selfless work and dedication, and his personal tolerance and foresight, even though, as he predicted, many further problems awaited him.

The Mandela administration (1994–1999) achieved impressive advances in establishing democracy and encouraging reconciliation, and in providing cheap housing, electricity, and clean water for millions of people in the black townships. It also secured economic stability inside the country and became a force, even a successful model, for peace around the world.

Mandela's primary role at this time was to achieve unity, both within the ANC and across the country as a whole. At the ANC's first national conference since assuming the reigns of political power, he carefully balanced competing demands for restitution of black rights with pragmatic requirements for economic growth in a globalizing world economy. If, by his own measure, the ANC would be judged on whether its decisions "bring practical relief to the millions" who supported it, then given the fact that business demands often appeared to outweigh "practical relief," Mandela could still point to national unity, peace, and stability as his government's crowning achievements.[5]

While apartheid was now dead, elements of its socioeconomic legacy persisted to limit the impact of Mandela's policies. Post-apartheid South Africa faced mammoth tasks: to consolidate democracy, lessen the social inequality inherited from 300 years of colonialism, and improve the day-to-day lives of the people. In general, enormous strides took place to achieve a measure of success in all these fields, for which Mandela can justly claim credit.

Democracy was Mandela's first major achievement. At first, he headed a government of national unity with both De Klerk and Thabo Mbeki serving as vice presidents. In 1996, De Klerk took the National Party out of government and the ANC governed in its own right. Two further successful national elections, in 1999 and 2004, confirmed the resilience of the multiparty democracy Mandela had championed, although some political analysts warned of the dangers of a "dominant party system" given the ANC's great electoral strength rooted in its historical leadership and in the country's demography. Nevertheless, South Africa developed a pluralistic state with well-established opposition parties, a vibrant civil society, and an independent press, all of which Mandela encouraged.

The newly elected Parliament sat first as a Constitutional Assembly, which created a Constitutional Court, comprising 11 independent judges. This court was empowered to certify a new constitution and ensure it complied with the Constitutional Principles agreed by negotiators. Mandela and his legal advisors encouraged a very wide process of public consultation to decide the sorts of principles a new constitution should embody.

The result was impressive. Many commentators view the new constitution eventually adopted in 1996 as the most forward-looking in the world. Unlike the apartheid-era "tricameral" Constitution of 1983 that institutionalized racial categories, the 1996 Constitution contains firm guarantees of equality. Underlying its principles (as in the U.S. Constitution) are equality, democracy, responsibility, and freedom, but also included are ideas of reconciliation and diversity. This Constitution, likely to be one of Mandela's greatest legacies, includes a Bill of Rights affirming human dignity, equality, and freedom. In addition, reflecting the recent times in which it appeared, the Constitution guarantees the right to basic and higher education, and adequate housing, the right to work and strike, the right of access to information, gender and sexual-persuasion rights, and protection of children and the environment. It asserts that "the state may not unfairly discriminate directly or indirectly against anyone on one or more grounds, including race, gender, sex, pregnancy, marital status, ethnic or social origin, colour, sexual orientation, age, disability, religion, conscience, belief, culture, language, and birth."[6]

Recent history had seen the growing role of women in politics. In 1984 the ANC had accepted "non-sexism" as part of its vision for a new South Africa. Mandela embraced this policy. In an interview in 2005, he recounted that while on Robben Island he had read widely of the growing role of women in politics around the world, and that this had reminded him of the role of the mother of the first Mandela, the founder of his clan, who had fought the British colonial invaders. As president, he soon adopted gender-neutral terms in his speeches. There is little doubt that African women massively supported Mandela and the ANC in national elections in 1994 and 1999, and that the 1996 Constitution is the most gender-sensitive in the world.[7]

The Mandela administration's achievements in the economy varied. The extension of housing, electricity, and clean water to a million poorer people, the right to land, free health care to pregnant women, and security for labor tenants were all substantial. As presidential initiatives, Mandela introduced a program of free milk for elementary school students and health care for mothers and children. All people were now free to live wherever they wished—if they could afford it. The government sought to create a more "level playing field" for black business and labor: it encouraged black economic empowerment, legalized strikes, and encouraged tripartite industrial conciliation between business, labor, and the state.

However, the pace of economic change was slow, with little appreciable redistribution of national wealth. In part, this was due to entrenched white power within the economy and the state apparatus. Mandela's cabinet made definite progress in the construction of a new, nonracial bureaucracy based on merit rather than race, but the commanding heights of the economy still remained largely in white hands and Mandela was loathe to precipitate capital flight by nationalization or by antagonizing the banks. In this regard, he succeeded in stemming capital flight.

Within the ANC and its electoral allies the Congress of South African Trade Unions and the South African Communist Party, which together formed the Tripartite Alliance, support was overwhelmingly for a redistribution of wealth in favor of the historically disadvantaged black majority. In accord with these popular demands, the Mandela government's initial economic policy framework, the Reconstruction and Development Program (RDP), built upon the traditional policies of the ANC (as outlined in the Freedom Charter) and its labor and political allies. The RDP envisaged such redistribution and social equality, but simultaneously sought to boost domestic capital accumulation.

However, under strong pressure from both corporate interests and ANC economic conservatives such as Thabo Mbeki, in 1996 Mandela agreed to replace the RDP with the pro-business (or "neoliberal") Growth, Employment, and Redistribution (GEAR) strategy. By 1999, Mandela's administration could boast of its strict financial management, low inflation, and the impressive elimination of the public debt of Rand 250 billion (in today's terms, about $35 billion; the rand is the South African currency). On the other hand, despite promises from the wealthy "North" (developed countries) of massive investment, this was modest. The personal goodwill extended to Mandela probably accounted for some inflow, but the failure of donors to invest on a large scale encouraged the new government to embrace other policies. Mandela also had to confront changing international approaches to aid: despite close relations, direct U.S. government aid to South Africa actually declined fourfold as Washington prioritized private investment instead.

Mandela's gamble on GEAR backfired in that a projected growth of 1.3 million jobs between 1996 and 2001 actually resulted in the loss of more than one million jobs. GEAR's projected growth and investment rates were not met. In contradiction to his 1994 election pledges, Mandela also decided to embrace privatization of state services. There was a sad irony here, when some poor Africans who had finally received clean water and electricity for the first time in their lives soon lost this access due to their inability to pay for newly privatized services. As privatization and globalization advanced, unemployment soared, with massive job losses in South Africa's key mining sector and other industries. Mandela and his ministers came up with various short-term job creation and poverty-reduction initiatives, but these had limited impact given entrenched white economic power and global markets, and Mandela's own reluctance to scare away business by seriously tackling the structural roots of black poverty. Instead he opted for a conservative "trickle-down" approach. Some critics claimed that economic power still resided among white corporate interests and that despite the growth of a new black elite stratum, ANC rule represented merely black empowerment for a tiny group; an "elite transition."[8]

Given the short time period of five years involved, vis-à-vis the gargantuan historical inequalities of South Africa, these criticisms can appear harsh. Running a country was not the same as leading a political party, and it involved compromises. Furthermore, although the ANC had won the election, many believed they were not quite able to secure real power.

Nevertheless, when considered from the point of view of the living conditions of the overwhelming majority of the population and their rising expectations, some of Mandela's macroeconomic decisions appear unwise in retrospect. South Africa's market economy, previously safeguarded by protectionism, was changing rapidly and was unable to absorb new workers or meet rising expectations. Undeniably, big business exerted considerable influence on Mandela. Their seductive overtures had begun in the transition period and steadily increased, and he had to decide one way or the other on the direction of future economic policy. Increasingly, as his authorized biographer observes, Mandela enjoyed the company of rich white businesspeople in Johannesburg's luxurious northern neighborhoods. Moreover, powerful globalization trends, the need for foreign investment, and low mineral prices, all encouraged Mandela to opt for fiscal prudence and neoliberal monetarist policies, and to compromise on the ANC's reform agenda. In this, he was strongly encouraged by Mbeki and the banks. Finally, the imposition of GEAR from above, rather than below, reflected the danger of a creeping antidemocratic trend that, if not the fault of any one person such as Mandela, remains a concern in present-day South Africa.[9]

Nelson Mandela the president had to face other serious problems. Land reform epitomizes post-apartheid compromise. Land dispossession lay at the heart of the inequality of colonial and apartheid South Africa: millions of blacks had lost their lands. Land reform therefore became a central ANC policy. Mandela made sure that the first legislation enacted after the watershed 1994 elections was the Restitution of Land Rights Act. Since then, there has been considerable, if slow and cumbersome, progress towards land restitution. In both rural and urban landscapes, the unequal infrastructure that is the physical legacy of apartheid undoubtedly will remain for some time, but Mandela at least made a start to an orderly process of compensation and legally binding land rights.

More menacing and apparently irresolvable has been the HIV-AIDS pandemic, which hit South Africa with all the shocking force of a colliding freight train. The causes of its rapid spread were rooted in factors such as virus transmission through transport routes, prostitution, and reluctance by traditionalists to embrace safe sex practices, while poverty exacerbated its impact. Mandela and his cabinet, naturally enough preoccupied with nation building and reconciliation, were too slow to perceive the growing magnitude of the problem to act decisively to reduce its spread.

The number of infected pregnant women rose from 0.7 percent in 1990, to 10.5 percent in 1995, and 22 percent in 1999, by which time an estimated four million people, or one-ninth of the entire population, were infected. Government funding scandals and differences between central and provincial administrations only made things worse. Mandela seemed unprepared, perhaps due to his generation and culture, to lead such a campaign personally, as had been the case with the presidents of the African countries of Uganda and Botswana. One medical researcher who raised the issue with Mandela early in his presidency found him courteous, but clearly preoccupied with the big political issues of the day. Probably the "greatest weakness" then of Mandela's leadership was this failure to lead the fight against the pandemic; over the following decade, as will be seen in the next chapter, he would seek to make amends.[10]

Despite these major problems, Mandela scored other impressive social victories. His boldest initiative to heal the deep divisions of the past was the Truth and Reconciliation Commission (TRC), probably the most widespread investigation into past injustices the world has ever known. Established by Mandela in 1995 under the Promotion of National Unity and Reconciliation Act and led at his insistence by fellow Nobel Peace Prize winner Archbishop Desmond Tutu, the TRC mandate from Mandela was to investigate gross human rights violations perpetrated between 1960 and 1993 to prevent them happening again and to unify a nation deeply divided by apartheid. Given a political motive for a crime and full, public testimony, then the TRC could offer amnesty to perpetrators. The exposure of atrocities in the dramatic proceedings of the commission, televised live, brought much pain to those involved but also had the cathartic power to help steer South Africa away from an endless cycle of violence in a boldly democratic direction.[11]

The TRC's emphasis on "restorative" rather than "retributive" justice related closely to the political compromises of the transition period that Mandela had pursued. The TRC did receive criticism, for example from the family of Steve Biko, for failing to bring to justice some of the worst perpetrators of crimes, and the reparations process was not particularly generous to victims' families. Despite such shortcomings, the proceedings had a therapeutic effect, enabling the country to transcend the violence of apartheid. A good measure of social reconciliation ensued and contributed to social peace and stability; the lessons to the world for conflict resolution were profound. Again, Mandela had achieved the seemingly impossible.[12]

In the field of reconciliation, Nelson Mandela led by personal example: his dramatic appearance in a Springbok jersey (that of team Captain François Pienaar) on the hallowed turf of Afrikaner rugby, Ellis Park, to join celebrations for South Africa's 1995 World Cup victory, and his drinking tea with the aging widow of the architect of apartheid, Verwoerd, epitomized reconciliation. Such gestures were a potent symbol to whites to leave behind the racial tensions of the past and work together with blacks to build a New South Africa.

In many other areas, Mandela and his administration left a lasting impact. Education and sports were steadily desegregated, culture freed from the shackles of apartheid censorship, and religious communities that had suffered under apartheid flourished. Rural development, road building, and environmental conservation measures expanded, and funds to combat poverty increased.

The heritage of South Africa also underwent transformation. In the past, museums had depicted the triumphal march of white settlers; there was little space for the stories of Africans. Symbolically, Mandela returned to Robben Island in September 1997 to launch on its soil a new kind of heritage museum devoted to all South Africans. "Let us," he stated, "recommit ourselves to the ideals in our Constitution, ideals which were shaped in the struggles here on Robben Island and in the greater prison that was apartheid South Africa."[13]

Mandela's long years of dutiful physical exercise and hard work stood him in good stead for the rigors of the presidency. In July 1994, he underwent eye surgery for a cataract, complicated by his experience of forced labor in the lime pits of Robben Island, but overall he displayed remarkable health for an octogenarian.

Mandela's personal and reflective style of government, characterized by some as consensual and by others as the "gracious patrician" in a "patriarchal meditative mode,"[14] could disarm his critics. If, as Constitutional Court judge Albie Sachs noted, Mandela was viewed by some as a "natural patriarch" and by others as a "a natural democrat," he was quick to adapt to the complicated public and private lives of a president. He disliked bureaucratic routine, and at times made unilateral decisions, but people seemed to forgive his cheerful impetuosity not least because he humanized government.[15]

Mandela's reputation as a great survivor and a person who eschewed bitterness for reconciliation, together with his dignity and warm personal style, captured the admiration of millions at home and abroad. Particularly endearing was his impish sense of humor and broad smile. Everything about him, from his slow meandering speeches, his wearing of colorful African shirts, and his ability even at the age of 80 to do a little impromptu African dance, evoked the image of the kindly grandfather, the father of the nation. In the glare of publicity accorded a president, Mandela "remained a star performer who could play all the parts: the African chief, the Western President, the sportsman, the philosopher, the jiver with the 'Madiba shuffle,'" and his dress shifted effortlessly from "dark suit to a loose flowery shirt to a rugby jersey to a T-shirt and baseball cap." At home and abroad, "Madiba magic" seemed to offer solutions to intractable problems.[16]

In external relations and foreign trade, Mandela scored further victories. Trade more than doubled during his presidency. Under Mandela's astute leadership, South Africa emerged from pariah status to become a respected "middle power" (such as, for example, Canada or Australia) capable of launching its own initiatives to combat world inequalities or to champion world peace.

Spearheading this new foreign policy was Mandela himself, "a giant" who strode the "world scene." He led several sorties aimed at bringing peace to troubled lands, including Northern Ireland, the Democratic Republic of the Congo, Angola, and Burundi. South Africa made major contributions to United Nations peace missions in Africa, actively supported nuclear disarmament, and secured election to major international bodies. South Africa under Mandela strongly endorsed human rights and ethics in international relations. It led the international campaign against the misery caused to civilians by land mines. In a speech at Oxford University in 1997, Mandela made an impassioned plea for peace: "Can we say with confidence that it is within our reach to declare that never again shall continents, countries or communities be reduced to the smoking battlefields of contending forces of nationality, religion, race, or language?"[17]

Mandela clearly recognized the importance of U.S. relations for South Africa. He established a very successful Bi-National Commission headed by Vice Presidents Gore and Mbeki, and in 1998 President Clinton made a successful visit to South Africa, the first ever by a serving U.S. president. In his address to the Joint Session of the U.S. Houses of Congress in September 1994, Mandela paid tribute to the "understanding among the millions of our people that here we have friends, here we have fighters against racism who feel hurt because we are hurt, who seek our success because they too seek the victory of democracy over tyranny." Yet friendship with one country did not mean to Mandela abandonment of "old friends" who had materially supported the ANC's struggle, such as Cuba and Libya. Here Mandela made use of his extensive contacts and his enormous personal moral capital to act successfully as a go-between to resolve the difficult problem of Libya and the Lockerbie bombing, a success that underscored his great skill as a mediator. On all foreign issues, he insisted that South Africa be independent, and nonaligned, and where he thought necessary he criticized U.S. policy, as over American pharmaceutical companies' refusal to supply cheap, generic AIDS drugs to South Africans. In general, however, U.S.-South African relations under Mandela reflected shared values and mutual interests.[18]

Mandela helped South Africa integrate into Africa. African countries had naturally kept their distance from the apartheid regime, but under Mandela, there was a rush on both sides to embrace new, friendly relations. Mandela strongly asserted South Africa's new identity as part of Africa, and also as part of the less developed "South." However, all was not smooth sailing for Mandela as African countries harbored suspicions that South Africa, with its greater economic power, might dominate. Although South African companies did rapidly expand their operations into Africa, Mandela encouraged his country to offer selfless assistance to neighbors, such as Mozambique and Angola, and to engage in mutually beneficial relations across the continent.

In some other foreign policy arenas, Mandela faced dilemmas. Taiwan had invested heavily in apartheid South Africa; it also wooed the ANC with large donations. However, China made clear it would not tolerate a "two Chinas" policy. After initially signaling that Pretoria would continue to trade with Taiwan, Mandela, who came to see Beijing's tremendous growth potential, changed course to recognize Beijing in 1998. Another controversial event was South Africa's military intervention in neighboring Lesotho, where clumsy efforts to reestablish democracy saw unnecessary loss of life.

Even more controversially, Mandela the advocate and harbinger of peace at home, who had cut defense spending by half, found himself supporting South Africa's large and profitable arms industry, built up under apartheid. Under his presidency, the industry continued to exports arms and profit from wars and destruction, posing the question of government priorities. Other controversies erupted over Mandela's hypocritical willingness to accept large donations to the ANC from dictators in Nigeria and Indonesia (see chapter 8). He pursued a delicate foreign policy with some African states. When in 1995 Nigerian dictator Abacha executed the writer and human rights activist Ken Saro-Wiwa, Mandela's policy of "quiet diplomacy" toward Nigeria within the Commonwealth backfired. When an outraged Mandela changed his tune, calling for stiff countermeasures, the lukewarm response by both Western and African countries, and by his vice president, Mbeki, disappointed him.

Beyond the glow of Mandela's rosy international reception, his personal life faced disruption. The final divorce with Winnie Madikizela-Mandela came in 1996 with considerable publicity and rancor. It was clear that both parties had lost their former love for each other. Each accused the other of neglect. In 1994, Mandela had briefly appointed Winnie a deputy minister, only to dismiss her after outspoken criticism of his government and controversial business operations. In the years since their separation, he had made extensive payments, rumored to amount to several million Rand, to cover her legal costs, but she refused an amicable settlement. In the divorce proceedings, she sought to exploit customary law, but Mandela retorted, "I respect custom, but I am not a tribalist." Finally, Winnie was legally obliged to vacate the family home.[19]

On July 18, 1998, his eightieth birthday, Mandela married Graça Machel. Born in 1945, she was the widow of the assassinated president of Mozambique, and had been active in charity work for refugees. Mandela had courted her persistently for years and found in her a political and cultural soul mate; he was, she said, "so easy to love." At the wedding reception, Mandela danced his "famous Madiba shuffle around the confetti-strewn dance floor." Remarriage eased the loneliness he had endured since the rupture with Winnie and the passing of many family members, such as his sister Leabie, who died in 1997.[20]

Mandela did not intend to monopolize power. In 1997, at the ANC's 50th annual congress, he handed over the ANC presidency to Thabo Mbeki, who two years later steered the movement to victory in South Africa's second democratic election. Over several years, Mandela had blooded Mbeki into the future role of president by stepping back from day-to-day tasks and letting the younger man assume important responsibilities.

Mandela left a rich legacy of splendid achievements and magnanimity. That he had inherited a complex country steeped in social and racial divisions with very different interest groups constantly jockeying for power partly explains some of the contradictory decisions he made in office. Yet as he stepped down from power, even at the age of 81, he did not intend to retire.

NOTES

1. Nelson Mandela, *Long Walk to Freedom: The Autobiography of Nelson Mandela* (Boston: Little, Brown, 1994), pp. 539–540.

2. "Celebrations Rock the Townships," *South* (Cape Town), May 6, 1994; Bill Keller, "Mandela Proclaims a Victory: South Africa Is 'Free At Last!'" *New York Times*, May 3, 1994.

3. Mandela, "Address to the Nation 10 May 1994," in *Nelson Mandela in His Own Words*, ed. Kader Asmal, David Chidester, and Wilmot James (New York: Little, Brown, 2003), p. 70.

4. "Mandela Story Breaks All Records," *Cape Times*, December 16, 1994; Mandela, *Long Walk to Freedom*, p. 544.

5. "Masterly Madiba," *Financial Mail* (Johannesburg), December 23, 1994, p. 27.

6. See the popular South African teaching resource, South African History Online http://www.sahistory.org.za/pages/sources/docs/doc37-bill-rights.htm.

7. Mac Maharaj and Ahmed Kathrada, *Mandela: The Authorized Portrait* (Kansas City, MO: Andrews McMeel, 2006), p. 343.

8. Patrick Bond, *Elite Transition: From Apartheid to Neoliberalism in South Africa* (Sterling, VA: Pluto Press, 2000), pp. 192–194; Sampie Terreblanche, *A History of Inequality in South Africa* (Pietermaritzburg: University of Natal Press, 2002), pp. 432–435; James Barber, *Mandela's World* (Athens: Ohio University Press, 2004), pp. 162–167.

9. Anthony Sampson, *Mandela: The Authorized Biography* (New York: Knopf, 1999), pp. 493, 506; Raymond Suttner, "African National Congress (ANC): Attainment of Power, Post Liberation Phases and Current Crisis," *Historia* (Pretoria) 52, no. 1, 2007: 1–46, p. 43.

10. Barber, *Mandela's World*, p. 136; Virginia van der Vliet, "South Africa Divided against AIDS: A Crisis of Leadership," and David Lindauer, "Challenges," in *AIDS and South Africa: The Social Expression of a Pandemic*, ed. Kyle Kauffman and David Lindauer (New York: Palgrave, 2004), pp. 48–96, and p. 178.

11. On the TRC proceedings, see the eminently readable Antjie Krog, *Country of My Skull* (New York: Random House, 1998), the documentary film *Long Nights Journey into Day*, which features American involvement, and the official TRC Web site: http://www.doj.gov.za/trc.

12. On the TRC see Steven D. Gish, *Desmond Tutu: A Biography* (Westport, CT: Greenwood Press, 2004), chapter 14; and Lyn Graybill, *Truth and Reconciliation in South Africa: Miracle or Model?* (Boulder, CO: Lynne Rienner, 2002).

13. Nelson Mandela, "The Heritage of Robben Island," in *Nelson Mandela in His Own Words*, p. 298.

14. Tom Lodge, *Mandela: A Critical Life* (New York: Oxford University Press, 2006), p. 222; Barber, *Mandela's World*, p. 87.

15. Albie Sachs, "Freedom in Our Lifetime," in *Nelson Mandela in his Own Words*, p. 57.

16. Sampson, *Mandela: The Authorized Biography*, p. 495.

17. Barber, *Mandela's World*, pp. 87, 152–162; *In the Words of Nelson Mandela*, p. 49.

18. *In the Words of Nelson Mandela*, p. 84; Barber, *Mandela's World*, pp. 144, 168.

19. Martin Meredith, *Nelson Mandela: A Biography* (New York: St. Martin's Press, 1998), p. 539; Lodge, *Mandela: A Critical Life*, p. 220.

20. Lodge, *Mandela: A Critical Life*, pp. 222–223; Maharaj and Kathrada, *Mandela: The Authorized Portrait*, p. 290.

Chapter 10

AFTER THE PRESIDENCY

It was a hard act to follow—from prisoner-for-life to president—but despite now being in his eighties Nelson Mandela continued to work for his country and for humanitarian causes after 1999, when Thabo Mbeki took over as president of South Africa.

The ANC under Thabo Mbeki continued Mandela's broad program to overcome the bitter legacy of apartheid and build a new South Africa. There was continued strong economic growth, including among the small but rising black elite, and the championing of peace and human rights abroad. However, these achievements could not mask enduring problems at home. The HIV-AIDS problem intensified. Mbeki went so far as denying the clinical evidence of the disease. His government did challenge transnational corporations to provide retroviral drugs more cheaply to South Africa, but vital years were lost while his government dithered over preferred treatments; his Minister of Health aroused international condemnation and derision when she favored the use of fruit juice and garlic over medically approved drugs.

Very high black unemployment and acute inequality remained another plague. Mbeki sought ways to mitigate poverty and unemployment, but many poor people continued to live in unhealthy and inadequate housing with irregular water and power services, the privatization of which made such necessities of life even more inaccessible. By now, government leaders had abandoned many of the ANC's earlier progressive social programs, echoing processes in other postcolonial African countries. Mbeki substituted in their place black pride through the "African Renaissance," a concept first mooted by Mandela.[1]

Notwithstanding these problems, the movement to which Mandela had devoted his life had achieved several outstanding victories, not least the ending of apartheid, the establishment of democracy, and the winning of three consecutive elections. Mandela could now look back on the previous five years as having realized his major life achievements.

Mandela was in some ways even more outspoken after leaving office. His continuing commitment to helping the weak animates the work of the Nelson Mandela Foundation, which assists children and HIV-AIDS sufferers. The "46664: Give One Minute of Your Life to AIDS" campaign referred to Mandela's prison number on Robben Island: he was prisoner number 466 of 1964. In 2002, he publicly embraced militant South African AIDS activist Zackie Achmat, and in July 2004 he addressed an International AIDS Conference in Thailand.

Madiba's newfound energy to combat the HIV-AIDS pandemic reflected his continuing commitment to his country and his people. He proudly wore an "I Am an HIV Treatment Supporter" T-shirt in public to show his solidarity with, and to help destigmatize, sufferers. In 2005, he tearfully but truthfully announced publicly that his own son, Makgatho, had died of the disease.

He maintained a busy work schedule and through the Nelson Mandela Foundation and the Nelson Mandela Children's Fund channeled resources to the disadvantaged. In 1994, Mandela had vowed to donate R150,000 of his presidential salary to children's welfare, and together with his new wife, Graça Machel, he intensified these efforts after leaving office, making good use of international events such as concerts to raise funds.

In his typically audacious and African patriarch's style, after publicly condemning the aggressive policies of the George W. Bush administration in Iraq as a "tragedy," Mandela called his father, George H. W. Bush, to admonish his son when the latter failed to reply to his telephone call. Conversely, if Mandela had become an international celebrity, then he was neither infallible nor above criticism. Mandela welcomed the doggedly persistent investigative journalist John Pilger, banned from South Africa by the apartheid regime in the 1960s, back there with a smile, and with a wisecrack that "to have been banned from my country is a great honor." When Pilger asked him point-blank about the financial support of Indonesian dictator Suharto for the ANC, Mandela asked Pilger if he thought he had perhaps been too soft on Suharto, conceding that such things were to him often "a dilemma." Pilger in turn could not but concede Mandela's grace.[2]

An event in July 2007 epitomizes Mandela's continued commitment to world peace and equality. He agreed to use his 89th birthday to mark the launch of a new elite group of retired public figures. In Johannes-burg, under the spreading canopy of a futuristic dome, "The Elders" of the global village, including former U.S. President Jimmy Carter, Archbishop Desmond Tutu, and former U.N. Secretary General Kofi Annan, vowed to address world problems. Mandela, although now frail and not expected to do a great deal on the committee, hoped that by "using their collective experience, their moral courage, and their ability to rise above nation, race, and creed," the little group could "make our planet a more peaceful and equitable place to live." Simultaneously, in Cape Town a star-studded "90 Minutes for Mandela" soccer match raised funds for humanitarian purposes. In September 2007, The Elders sent a peace delegation to con-flict-ridden Darfur. The idea of The Elders had originated from British billionaire Richard Branson and rock star Peter Gabriel, but the notion of "the wisdom of the elders" clearly resonated with Mandela's own African culture.[3]

No one can either doubt the sincerity of such projects or not marvel at the continued commitment of Mandela to a better world. Yet, realisti-cally, whether current or future world leaders would even deign to listen to such a group or still less, act on its recommendations is problematic. Here the dynamic tension in Mandela's life work between his great strug-gles for righteous causes and the external forces that often impeded him is apparent. More cynical observers might even question the elitist nature of The Elders and ask whether Mandela, and those who make use of his good name, have purposively cultivated the image of Mandela the elder states-person while neglecting other, more broad-based forms of consultation equally embedded in both African and Western democratic traditions. In any case, Mandela's great struggle for a righteous cause continues and will continue into the future as part of his legacy.

In 2006, at the venerable age of 88, Mandela finally conceded that he had officially retired and declined further interviews. There were rumors that the South African government had asked him to stop commenting publicly on controversial issues, especially the AIDS epidemic. Mandela the elder, despite periodic requests for his presence, now had more time to devote to his family. In Graça, he had found much more than a new companion; she shared his vision for a better world. The adjustment from lifetime political prisoner had brought problems of adjustment to new life-styles. Mandela and his fellow ex-prisoners "found it difficult to adjust to our new family situations." The families had to get on with their liv-ing and "We were unable to dance with them." Yet behind this familial gulf, there was the logic of history. "Our vision of a future for our people blinded us to any other view. And perhaps that's the way it has to be." But now, with Graça at his side, Mandela could savor the delights of family life and enjoy the company of his many grandchildren.[4]

There was time now to spend between the city and the country. In his home village of Qunu, a new, modest Mandela Museum arose. The wheel of life had turned full circle. Mandela had returned, after years of adventure and toil, first in the 1940s in the City of Gold among black miners and radical activists, then from the 1950s living the dangerous life of the underground and prison, finally to lead the "miracle" of South Africa's democratic transformation. Now he could bask in the patrician aura once enjoyed by his noble forebears.

Over the years, as noted in Chapter 7, the world had bestowed upon Nelson Mandela numerous awards and high honors, with streets, schools, and parks named in his honor. They would take many pages just to list, but besides the 1993 Nobel Peace Prize, the International Gandhi Peace Prize, and numerous honorary doctorates, in 2002 he received the Presidential Medal of Freedom, the United States' highest civilian award.[5]

Nelson Mandela's legacy to South Africa, Africa, and the world is immense. He was, as his successor Thabo Mbeki notes, "A child of the ANC."[6] Mandela would be the first to agree that overcoming 300 years of a very different—a colonial—legacy was always a joint effort spearheaded by the movement to which he devoted his life. Yet, if it was Mandela the team player who united and lead the ANC then it was Mandela the individual who initiated negotiations and who secured the moral high ground in the crucial transition period. He did so by personal example, by the exemplary nature of his character, his suffering, and his magnanimous forgiving of old enemies. Mandela's deft combination of his personal gifts with the organizational appeal of the ANC is the key to understanding his success as a politician.

Always, Mandela's motivation was freedom and a better life for his people; if in the 1930s this meant the Thembu or Xhosa, by the 1950s it had widened to include all Africans and later to embrace South Africans of all races and political persuasions, including his former political enemies.

His greatest legacy to South Africa is freedom and a working, stable democracy, a humane and entirely modern constitution, and a solid start on the long road to reconciliation and equitable socioeconomic development. His legacy to Africa and the world is renewed hope in the power amicably to resolve deep-seated conflicts and to leave behind forever the hatred of racism and war.

The accomplishments of Mandela's relatively brief administration from 1994 to 1999 are considerable. Firstly, he helped bring peace to a country ravaged by decades of civil conflict and on the verge of civil war. Second, he ushered in democracy and freedom for blacks after 300 years of authoritarian colonialism, land dispossession, and racism. Third, Mandela's government made substantial progress in the direction of redressing such inherited problems and moving on toward a plural and more tolerant society, in the manner of the Truth and Reconciliation Commission and land reform. Fourth, the living conditions for the majority of the people improved with the provision of hundreds of thousands of new houses, electricity provision to millions of Africans, and the establishment of nonracial socioeconomic structures and peace. Perhaps most of all, a new South Africa emerged, which if it still carried the burden of the past in terms of social inequalities and stereotypes of race, now embraced Mandela's vision of a free society based on a democratic, nonracial constitution.

Yet Mandela's legacy extends even beyond these great achievements. He had rescued South Africa's international reputation from being a "polecat among nations" to a well-respected international partner that was a model of successful conflict resolution. He had played a role in brokering peace accords in the conflict-ridden countries of Burundi and the Democratic Republic of the Congo. On the world stage, Mandela had worked hard to foster peaceful relations between different peoples.

Over and above all these achievements looms something intangible yet perhaps more effective: the example of a life spent struggling against adversity, imprisonment, and racism and yet marked by wonderful magnanimity, of a spirit not of revenge for past injustices but of reconciliation and forgiveness to enable progress in building a better world. In this regard, the name Nelson Mandela has come to be synonymous with the endurance of the human spirit, of victory over evil.

Archbishop Desmond Tutu remarked that, as Martin Luther King took the struggle for civil rights "beyond the civil rights era to what he called the poor people's movements," then so Mandela has become "a beacon of peace and hope for millions." Nigerian writer and Nobel Laureate Wole Soyinka, a fellow fighter for human rights who also spent years in a political prison and is perhaps Africa's leading playwright, described Mandela as a symbol of the spirit of humanity's dialogue for a rainbow culture, a person of "unparalleled generosity of spirit." African American writer Cornell West portrayed Mandela as "great exemplar of the grand democratic tradition." Former U.S. President Bill Clinton characterized Mandela's struggle as one purified by the severe trials he endured such that, as president, Mandela brought into government even his enemies, to try "to get all South Africans to make the same 'long walk to freedom' that has made his own life so extraordinary."[7]

Mandela's bequest is not just political—in the form of South African's successful democracy, or economic—in the form of a growing black renaissance. The spirit of freedom enjoyed by South Africans today is no less significant for its intangible nature. This legacy is being realized practically if modestly at a grassroots level through his charitable foundations such as the Nelson Mandela Foundation and the Nelson Mandela Children's Fund. August 2007 saw the launch of the Nelson Mandela Institute for Education and Rural Development in South Africa's impoverished Eastern Cape region. Backed by the Nelson Mandela Foundation and by Mandela's old college, the University of Fort Hare, and South Africa's Education Department, the institute aims to inject millions of dollars for a new rural education program and is just one manifestation of Mandela's ongoing commitment to his country.

For Mandela it has been a lifetime of struggle; there was "no easy walk to freedom"; it was truly a very "long walk to freedom." To overcome the tremendous, seemingly insurmountable barriers in the way to this freedom required a great movement of peoples, and great leaders. Mandela devoted his life to the ANC as the vehicle for the freedom of all South Africans. He could not have made it without them; they could not have made it without one such as him. His determination, brilliance, energy, and endurance, and above all his character, were major factors in securing the end of apartheid and the gains of the New South Africa. As his longtime friend on Robben Island, Eddie Daniels, put it, Nelson Mandela "is quite simply one of the greatest persons in human history."[8]

NOTES

1. Sampie Terreblanche, *A History of Inequality in South Africa* (Pietermaritzburg, South Africa: University of Natal Press, 2002); William M. Gumede, *Thabo Mbeki and the Battle for the Soul of the ANC* (Cape Town: Zebra Press, 2005).

2. John Pilger, *Freedom Next Time* (London: Bantam, 2006), p. 259.

3. "Former Leaders Create Freelance Global Diplomatic Team," *New York Times,* July 18, 2007, and "Mandela's Elders to Tackle Global Crises," *Guardian Weekly,* July 27, 2007. See http://www.theelders.org/.

4. Nelson Mandela, Foreword to Padraig O'Malley, *Shades of Difference: Mac Maharaj and the Struggle for South Africa* (New York: Viking, 2007), p. 17.

5. For a list of awards, see http://www.anc.org.za/ancdocs/history/mandela/awards/.

6. Mac Maharaj and Ahmed Kathrada, *Mandela: The Authorized Portrait* (Kansas City, MO: Andrews McMeel, 2006), p. 291.

7. Desmond Tutu, Wole Soyinka, and Cornell West in *The Meaning of Mandela: A Literary and Intellectual Celebration*, ed. Xolela Mangcu (Cape Town: HSRC Press, 2006), pp. ix, 13, 33; William J. Clinton, Foreword to *Nelson Mandela in His Own Words*, p. xv.

8. Eddie Daniels, interview with the author, October 13, 2006, East Lansing, MI.

GLOSSARY

African National Congress (ANC)—Founded in 1912, the major African nationalist movement, which since 1994 has governed South Africa.

African nationalism—A political philosophy based on achieving independence for Africans subjected to colonial rule or asserting African sovereignty.

Afrikaners—South African white minority (7 percent of the total population, but a majority of whites) who speak the Afrikaans language and trace descent from Dutch settlers.

Apartheid—Policy of legalized extreme racial discrimination, implemented from 1948, finally uprooted in 1994; from the Afrikaans "separateness" or "apartness."

Bantu Education—An apartheid policy, first introduced in the 1950s, which imposed inferior education on Africans.

Bantustans—Ethnic "homelands" forcibly imposed on Africans by the apartheid regime.

Congress of South African Trade Unions (COSATU)—The major South African labor federation, in electoral alliance with the ANC.

Congress Youth League—Established 1944, with Mandela as cofounder; in 1949 replaced ineffective ANC strategy with vigorous protest policies.

Convention for a Democratic South Africa (CODESA)—Negotiating forum established in December 1991 to draft new constitution; deadlocked, May 1993.

Defiance Campaign—Large-scale, nationwide protests against discriminatory apartheid laws in 1952 that led to the ANC becoming a mass-based organization.

Freedom Charter—Policy program adopted by the Congress of the People in 1955, and subsequently the ANC's chief program until 1996.

Group Areas Act (1950)—A central pillar of apartheid legislation forcing blacks to live in segregated areas.

Growth, Employment, and Redistribution (GEAR)—The Mandela administration's second economy policy, which in 1996 replaced the RDP.

Inkatha Freedom Party—Sectional (Zulu) political party led by Mangosuthu Buthelezi.

National Party—Political party supported mainly by Afrikaners, in power 1948 to 1994.

Pan Africanist Congress (PAC)—Breakaway party from the ANC, founded in 1959.

Pass laws—A series of rigid laws and statutes restricting the free movement, work, and living areas of Africans in South Africa, gradually phased out from the 1980s.

Rand—South African currency.

Reconstruction and Development Program (RDP)—Mandela administration's initial economic policy, 1994–1995, replaced by GEAR.

Rivonia Trial—Trial for sabotage, lasting from 1963 to 1964, which resulted in the sentencing to life imprisonment of Mandela and his co-accused.

Robben Island—Prison off Cape Town incarcerating Mandela from 1964 to 1982.

South African Communist Party (SACP)—Formed in 1921, banned in 1950, relaunched underground in mid-1950s, then legally in 1990; electoral ally of ANC.

Soweto—Huge, sprawling township southwest of Johannesburg where Mandela lived in the 1940s and 1950s; the initial site of the Youth Revolt of 1976.

Transkei—Literally, "Across the Kei" (River), the region where Mandela was born.

Treason Trial—A mass trial of 156 anti-apartheid leaders, including Mandela, from 1956–1961, which resulted in the complete exoneration of all the accused.

Truth and Reconciliation Commission (TRC)—1995–1998, chaired by Desmond Tutu, to expose human rights violations and heal apartheid wounds.

***Umkhonto we Sizwe* (MK, "Spear of the Nation")**—Military organization of the ANC founded in 1961 by Mandela; integrated into South African army after 1994.

United Democratic Front (UDF)—Very wide coalition of civic, church, labor, and political organizations, formed in 1983 and broadly supportive of the ANC.

Xhosa—A major South African nationality; also the language spoken by Xhosa people, including Nelson Mandela.

Zulu—A major South African nationality; the language spoken by Zulu people.

SELECTED BIBLIOGRAPHY

SELECTION OF PUBLISHED WORKS BY NELSON MANDELA

In His Own Words. Edited by Kader Asmal, David Chidester, and Wilmot James. New York: Little, Brown, 2003.

In the Words of Nelson Mandela. Edited by Jennifer Crwys-Williams. New York: Penguin, 1997.

Long Walk to Freedom: The Autobiography of Nelson Mandela. Boston: Little, Brown, 1994.

Mandela: An Illustrated Autobiography. Boston: Little, Brown, 1996.

No Easy Walk to Freedom. New York: Penguin, 2002.

The Struggle Is My Life. London: International Defence and Aid Fund, 1990.

BOOKS

Barber, James. *Mandela's World: The International Dimension of South Africa's Political Revolution 1990–99.* Athens: Ohio University Press, 2004.

Benson, Mary. *A Far Cry.* New York: Viking Penguin, 1989.

———. *Nelson Mandela.* New York: W. W. Norton, 1986 (updated 1994).

———. *South Africa; the Struggle for a Birthright.* London: IDAF, 1985.

Buntman, Fran Lisa. *Robben Island and Prisoner Resistance to Apartheid.* New York: Cambridge University Press, 2003.

Callinicos, Luli. *Oliver Tambo: Beyond the Engeli Mountains.* Cape Town: D. Philip, 2004.

———. *The World That Made Mandela: A Heritage Trail.* Johannesburg: STE, 2000.

Daniels, Eddie. *There and Back: Robben Island 1964–1979*. Cape Town, South Africa: Mayibuye, 1998.

Dingake, Michael. *My Fight against Apartheid*. London: Kliptown Books, 1987,

Gilbey, Emma. *The Lady: The Life and Times of Winnie Mandela*. London: Cape, 1993.

Gish, Steven. *Alfred B. Xuma: African, American, South African*. New York: New York University Press, 1999.

———. *Desmond Tutu: A Biography*. Westport, CT: Greenwood Press, 2004.

Guiloineau, Jean. *The Early Life of Rolihlahla Madiba Nelson Mandela*. Berkeley, CA: North Atlantic Books, 1998.

Harrison, Nancy. *Winnie Mandela: Mother of a Nation*. London: Gollancz, 1985.

Huddleston, Trevor. *Naught for Your Comfort*. New York: Doubleday, 1956.

Johns, Sheridan, and R. Hunt Davis Jr., eds. *Mandela, Tambo and the ANC: The Struggle against Apartheid*. New York: Oxford University Press, 1991.

Kathrada, Ahmed. *Letters from Robben Island: A Selection of Ahmed Kathrada's Prison Correspondence, 1964–1989*. Edited by Robert Vassen. East Lansing: Michigan State University Press, 1999.

———. *Memoirs*. Cape Town: Zebra Press, 2004.

Kerr, Alexander. *Fort Hare 1915–48: The Evolution of an African College*. New York: Humanities Press, 1968.

Krog, Antjie. *Country of My Skull*. New York: Random House, 1998.

Kumalo, Alf. *Mandela: Echoes of an Era*. New York: Viking Penguin, 1990.

Lodge, Tom. *Mandela: A Critical Life*. New York: Oxford University Press, 2006.

Magubane, Peter. *Nelson Mandela, Man of Destiny: A Pictorial Biography*. Cape Town: Nelson, 1996.

Maharaj, Mac, ed., *Reflections in Prison*. Cape Town: Robben Island Museum, 2001.

Maharaj, Mac, and Ahmed Kathrada. *Mandela: The Authorized Portrait*. Kansas City, MO: Andrews McMeel, 2006.

Mandela, Winnie. *Part of My Soul Went with Him*. New York: Viking Penguin, 1985.

Mangcu, Xolela, ed. *The Meaning of Mandela: A Literary and Intellectual Celebration*. Cape Town: HSRC Press, 2006.

Meer, Fatima. *Higher than Hope: The Authorized Biography of Nelson Mandela*. Revised ed. New York: Harper, 1990.

Meer, Ismail. *A Fortunate Man*. Cape Town: Zebra Press, 2002.

Meredith, Martin. *Nelson Mandela: A Biography*. New York: St. Martin's Press, 1998.

Naidoo, Indres. *Robben Island: Ten Years As a Political Prisoner in South Africa's Most Notorious Penitentiary*. New York: Vintage, 1983.

Nelson Mandela Foundation. *A Prisoner in the Garden*. New York: Viking Studio, 2006.

O'Malley, Padraig. *Shades of Difference: Mac Maharaj and the Struggle for South Africa*. New York: Viking, 2007.

Peires, J. B. *The House of Phalo: A History of the Xhosa People in the Days of Their Independence*. Berkeley: University of California Press, 1982.

The Road to Democracy in South Africa. Cape Town: Zebra Press, 2004.

Sampson, Anthony. *Mandela: The Authorized Biography*. New York: Knopf, 1999.

Sisulu, Elinor. *Walter and Albertina Sisulu: In Our Lifetime*. Cape Town: D. Philip, 2002.

Sisulu, Walter. *I Will Go Singing: Walter Sisulu Speaks of His Life and the Struggle for Freedom in South Africa*. Cape Town: Robben Island Museum, 2001.

Sparks, Allister. *Tomorrow Is Another Country: The Inside Story of South Africa's Road to Change*. New York: Hill and Wang, 1995.

Thompson, Leonard. *The Political Mythology of Apartheid*. New Haven, CT: Yale University Press, 1985.

Walshe, Peter. *The Rise of African Nationalism in South Africa: The African National Congress, 1912–1952*. Berkeley: University of California Press, 1971.

PERIODICALS

Keller, Bill. "Mandela Proclaims a Victory: South Africa Is 'Free At Last!'" *New York Times*, May 3, 1994.

Limb, Peter. "Early ANC Leaders and the British World: Ambiguities and Identities," *Historia* 47, no. 1, 2002: 56–82.

Maluleke, Elias. "Mandela: Can He Save South Africa?" *Pace*, March 1990: 6–16.

Suttner, Raymond. "African National Congress (ANC): Attainment of Power, Post Liberation Phases and Current Crisis," *Historia* 52, no. 1, 2007: 1–46.

INTERNET SOURCES

"Biography of Nelson Mandela." http://www.anc.org.za/people/mandela.html.

"The Long Walk of Nelson Mandela." http://www.pbs.org/wgbh/pages/frontline/shows/mandela.

"Mandela: An Audio History." http://www.radiodiaries.org/mandela/mpeople.html.

"The Mandela Page." http://www.anc.org.za/people/mandela/index.html.

"Nelson Mandela Biography" (South Africa History Online). http://www.sahistory.org.za/.

FILMS

The Long Walk of Nelson Mandela. Alexandria, VA: PBS Home Video, 1999.

Madiba: The Life and Times of Nelson Mandela. Canada: CBC, 2004.

Mandela: Free at Last. Woodland Hills, CA: Globalvision, 1990.

Mandela in America. New York: Vision Entertainment, 1990.

Mandela: Son of Africa, Father of a Nation. Johannesburg: Island Pictures, 1995.

OTHER

Cape Archives Repository, Cape Town.

Carter Karis Collection, Center for Research Libraries, Chicago.

Colin Tatz, interview with the author, Sydney, Australia, August 9, 2005.

Eddie Daniels, interview with the author, East Lansing, MI, October 13, 2006.

Kathrada Collection, Michigan State University Library.

Malcolm Fraser, telephone interview with the author, March 26, 2006.

Mandela family interviews, Peter Davis Collection, Indiana University.

INDEX

About the Author

PETER LIMB is Africana bibliographer and associate professor (adjunct) of history at Michigan State University, East Lansing. He specializes in South African history and African studies bibliography.